—

Corporate Governance and Resource Security in China

Routledge Studies in Corporate Governance

Corporate Governance and Resource Security in China

The Transformation of China's
Global Resources Companies

Xinting Jia and Roman Tomasic

Routledge
Taylor & Francis Group
New York   London

First published 2010
by Routledge
711 Third Ave, New York, NY 10017

Simultaneously published in the UK
by Routledge
2 Park Square, Milton Park, Abingdon, Oxon OX14 4RN

Routledge is an imprint of the Taylor & Francis Group, an informa business

Typeset in Sabon by IBT Global.

Library of Congress Cataloging-in-Publication Data
Xinting, Jia.
    Corporate governance and resource security in China : the transformation of China's global resources companies / by Xinting Jia and Roman Tomasic.
        p. cm. — (Routledge studies in corporate governance)
    Includes bibliographical references and index.
    1. Corporate governance—China. I. Tomasic, Roman. II. Title.
    HD2741.X55 2009
    338.60951—dc22
    2009016460

ISBN10: 0-415-45325-9 (hbk)
ISBN10: 0-203-86936-2 (ebk)

ISBN13: 978-0-415-45325-7 (hbk)
ISBN13: 978-0-203-86936-9 (ebk)

This book is dedicated by Dr Xinting Jia to her late father who had guided her until his last days of life

Contents

Figures

Tables

Abbreviations

ABS   Australian Bureau of Statistics

ADRs   American Depository Receipts

ARA   Australian Reporting Award

ASA   Australian Shareholder Association

ASC   Australian Securities Commission

ASIC   Australian Securities and Investments Commission

ASX   Australian Securities Exchange

BRW   Business Review Weekly

CCP   Chinese Communist Party

CEO   chief executive officer

CFO   chief financial officer

Chalco   Aluminum Corporation of China Limited

Chinalco   Aluminum Corporation of China

CNOOC   China National Offshore Oil Corporation

CNPC   China National Petroleum Corporation

CPPCC   Chinese People's Political Consultative Conference

CRA   Conzinc Riotinto of Australia

CSG   customer services group

CSGs   customer sector groups

CSR	corporate social responsibility
CSRC	China Securities Regulatory Commission
DJSI	Dow Jones Sustainability World Indexes
DLC	dual-listed company
EITI	Extractive Industries Transparency Initiative
ESG	environmental, social and governance
ESHIA	environmental, social and health impact assessment
ESOP	employee stock ownership program
FIRB	Foreign Investment Review Board
GRI	Global Reporting Initiative
HSEC	health, safety, environment and community
IAG	International Advisory Group
IFC	International Finance Corporation
MBO	management buyout .
MOSOP	Movement for the Survival of the Ogoni People
NGOs	not-for-profit organizations
OECD	Organisation for Economic Co-operation and Development
PNG	Papua New Guinea
PNGSDP	Papua New Guinea Sustainable Development Program
PRC	People's Republic of China
PRI	Principles for Responsible Investment
QFII	Qualified Foreign Institutional Investor
RTZ	Rio Tinto-Zinc Corporation
SASAC	State-owned Assets Supervision and Administration Commission
SEC	Securities and Exchange Commission

SETC   State Economic and Trade Commission

SGBP   Shell General Business Principles

Shell   Royal Dutch Shell

Sinopec   China Petroleum & Chemical Corporation

SIRAN   Social Investment Research Analyst Network

SOE(s)   state-owned enterprise(s)

WTO   World Trade Organisation

UNEP   United Nations Environment Programme

Foreword

It took less than twenty years for China's stock market to grow into a major emerging market from its inception in 1990. However, it has been a rather emotional ride for both investors and regulators. Not only has the stock market experienced dramatic ups and downs over the years, China has also not been short of its own version of "Enrons" and "Worldcoms."

The determination by the Government of China to reform corporate governance and improve investor confidence led to the issue of *The Code for Corporate Governance for Listed Companies in China* in 2002. While the Code has to a certain extent helped to improve corporate governance in listed companies, there is a general consensus that further improvement can only be achieved through better understanding of how corporate governance is really practiced at firm level.

This book is timely in addressing this theme as it focuses on corporate governance practices at firm level. Specifically, it has been focused on corporate governance in leading resources companies that are of critical importance to the further development of the Chinese economy. This book is based on interviews with controllers of leading resources companies and provides insights into how these companies are really managed at firm level. Comparisons are made with international practices in other leading resources companies in Australia, the United States and Europe. The authors also discuss the themes of corporate social responsibility and resource security, which are major concerns related to resources companies in the mining and oil industries.

This is not only a thought-provoking book but also essential reading for those who are new to the Chinese stock market. I highly recommend it to corporate governance professionals, including controllers and regulators, as well as resources sector specialists who want to gain an in-depth understanding of how corporate governance works in companies in this industry.

Professor Ruyin Hu
Director of Research
Shanghai Stock Exchange

Acknowledgments

From Dr. Xinting Jia: First of all, I would like to pay tribute to my father, who was my best friend and great mentor. He always encouraged me to pursue goals in my life. His perseverance and positive attitude to life will always light my path for the rest of my life. Dad, I am always missing you. This book would not be possible without the support of my family, my mom's love, my sister Xintong's encouragement and my husband Yong Tian's day-to-day support. Playing with my son Alan provided me with the much-needed break between writings and the inspiration to dive into it again! I would also like to thank my parents-in-law for their support; without their help, I would not have been able to produce this book while working full time.

Professor Roman Tomasic would like to thank all of those who participated in this study and gave their time and expertise to better inform us.

The authors would also like to thank the members of the research team that made this project possible; these included Professor Neil Andrews and Dr. Jane Fu, who were co-principal investigators with Professor Roman Tomasic on the larger research project out of which this book grew; we would also like to acknowledge three Chinese research officers who helped to make the project happen; their names are not mentioned here so as to protect them from our errors and misinterpretations. We would also like to thank the staff at the Centre for International Corporate Governance Research of Victoria University, Professor Anona Armstrong, Ms. Vicky Totikidis and Professor Ronald Francis, for their continuing support.

This book is based on Dr. Xinting Jia's PhD thesis. Some of this book's chapters are also rewritten based substantially on published material by Dr. Xinting Jia. Permission to republish those materials has been obtained from editors of journals and conference proceedings. The titles of the chapters and the published articles they are based on are listed as follows: a section of Chapter 2 is based on "Governing China's listed companies: annual reports and the role of the PRC Code of corporate governance," *Australian Journal of Corporate Law*, vol. 18, no. 3, pp. 233–242; a section of Chapter 3 is based on "Corporate governance in the resources sector in China and Australia," in Wu, Y. and Yu, C. (eds.), *The Chinese Economy: Trade, Reforms, Corporate Governance and Regional Development*, University of Western Australia, Perth, 2006; Chapter 7 has used some material from "Corporate governance and corporate social responsibility in China: past, present and future," *Australian Journal of Corporate Law*, vol. 17, no. 1, pp. 136–143. The authors would like to thank the publishers for their support and patience during the preparation of the manuscript.

The authors would also like to acknowledge that the findings and opinions in this book are based only on the authors' personal views.

1 The Rise of Large Resources Companies in China

INTRODUCTION

China's phenomenal economic growth has moved it towards being a new world superpower alongside the United States. In the seven years since 2000, China has managed to achieve an average 10% growth each year (Hyland, 2008). The continued growth in China has also put an enormous demand pressure on energy and natural resources, such as oil, gas and metals. Along with the increasing demand on natural resources, China has witnessed the rise and the growth of its resources sector companies which have increasingly played a significant role in China's economy.

In recent years, the rise of China has seen an increase in research on China due to relatively poor understanding of it by the outside world. Despite this increasing body of research, relatively little is known of its resources sector. This book seeks to fill some of these gaps by providing an analysis of resources sector firms in China. In particular, it looks closely at the corporate governance of these resources companies, operating in the context of China's unique political, social and economic environment.

While resources companies in China have in many ways learned from co-operating with leading resources companies around the world, increasingly these Chinese companies are also comparing themselves with foreign companies in similar industries. However, Chinese resources companies are in many aspects quite different in nature from their foreign counterparts. This book brings a fresh perspective to our understanding of China's major resources companies, such as oil companies Sinopec, PetroChina, China National Offshore Oil Corporation (CNOOC), and metals industry companies Aluminum Corporation of China (Chalco) and Baosteel. Based on in-depth interviews with senior company officers and government officials in China, this book also examines the role of the Chinese government in shaping resources companies and to what extent these companies have in practice adopted international corporate governance practices.

Case studies of the world's leading resources giants such as BHP Billiton, Rio Tinto, Shell and Chevron are provided to allow a comparison to be made. Case studies of Sinopec and Baosteel are also provided to further demonstrate the development of corporate governance at the firm level and to enhance our understanding of the changes now occurring in resources companies in China. In addition, this book addresses contemporary issues of resource security, environmental change and corporate social responsibility; these are of considerable significance in relation to China's strategically important resources companies.

To facilitate our understanding of corporate governance structures and practices in resources companies, Chapter 1 provides some brief background discussion of the historical development of China's resources companies after Mao's death in 1976; in Chapter 2, this book discusses the regulatory environment of resources companies and how regulatory forces have contributed to the current governance arrangements found in these companies.

Chapter 3 provides an analysis of corporate governance practices in major resources companies in China using resources companies in Australia as a point of comparison. Australia is a resource-rich country and houses a number of the world's largest resources companies (BHP Billiton and Rio Tinto). The current resources boom in Australia can largely be attributed to the enormous demand for natural resources from China, and so far, Australian-based resources companies and Australia's national economy have been major beneficiaries of a fast-growing Chinese economy (The Economist, 2008).

Chapter 4 is based on interviews with Chinese company directors, company secretaries and government officials and provides further insights into governance practices in China in the resources sector. Chapters 5 illustrates corporate governance practices in the world's leading resources companies by providing case studies of BHP Billiton, Rio Tinto, Shell and Chevron. Chapter 6 substantiates governance structures in Chinese resources companies by presenting case studies on Sinopec and Baosteel and demonstrates similarities and differences in their corporate governance practices when compared with those of the leading resources companies examined in Chapter 5.

Given the unique characteristics of corporate governance in China, the role of the government in controlling and regulating listed companies (including these in the resources sectors) has been significant; this has been highlighted by the controversy that has embroiled Chinese resources firms trying to control natural resources overseas through takeovers. Chapter 7 therefore explores the implications of a resource-hungry China for resource security in a global context. Chapter 8 further examines corporate governance and corporate social responsibility under the unique regulatory environment found in China, with a focus on environmental issues. Chapter 9 summarizes key arguments in this book and offers thoughts on future development in this area.

THE RISE OF LARGE RESOURCES COMPANIES IN CHINA

China's rapid economic growth in recent years has facilitated the rise of the resources sector firms in China. Since 2001, *Fortune* magazine started to publish a list of China's top 100 companies. In the 2004 *Fortune* listing, many firms belonging to the metals, petroleum and gas industries had risen higher from their 2003 rankings (Fortune China, 2004). In 2004, the composition of the top 100 listed companies in China was heavily tilted toward the resources sector, due largely to China's rapid economic development; this development has also served as a driving force stimulating the rise of the resources sector.

Among the top 100 listed companies in China in 2004, 35 companies belonged to the resources sector, namely, metals, petroleum and gas, and mining; these are listed in Table 1.1.

Table 1.1 Companies That Belonged to the Resources Sector in 2003 from List of Top 100 Companies

Ranking*	Chinese company name
1	China Petroleum & Chemical Corporation (Sinopec)
2	PetroChina Company Limited
8	Minmetals Development Co., Ltd.
9	Baoshan Iron & Steel Co., Ltd.
10	CNOOC Limited
12	Sinopec Shanghai Petrochemical Company Limited
13	Sinopec Zhenhai Refining & Chemical Company Limited
18	Aluminum Corporation of China Limited (Chalco)
19	Sinopec Yangzi Petrochemical Co., Ltd.
20	Jilin Chemical Industrial Co., Ltd.
24	Shanxi Taigang Stainless Steel Co., Ltd.
28	Maanshan Iron & Steel Company Limited
29	Beijing Shougang Co., Ltd.
32	Angang New Steel Co., Ltd.
35	Tangshan Iron & Steel Co., Ltd.
43	Hunan Valin Steel Tube and Wire Co., Ltd.
44	Handan Iron & Steel Co., Ltd.
50	Sinopec Beijing Yanhua Petrochemical Company Limited
51	Bengang Steel Plates Co., Ltd.
54	Jinzhou Petrochemical Co., Ltd.
55	Sinochem International Co., Ltd.
57	Laiwu Steel Co., Ltd.
59	Inner Mongolian Baotou Steel Union Co., Ltd.
60	Sinopec Yizheng Chemical Fibre Company Limited
67	Sinopec Qilu Co., Ltd.
68	Anyang Iron & Steel Inc.
69	Panzhihua New Steel & Vanadium Co., Ltd.
71	Yanzhou Coal Mining Company Limited
74	Sinopec Kantons Holdings Limited
79	Hangzhou Iron & Steel Co., Ltd.
81	SGIS Songshan Co., Ltd.
87	Nanjing Iron & Steel Co., Ltd.
89	Wuhan Steel Processing Company Limited
92	Guangzhou Iron & Steel Co., Ltd.
99	Shijiazhuang Refining-Chemical Co., Ltd.

*Note: the companies were ranked according to their revenue in 2003.
Source: (*Fortune* China 2004).

Among these 35 companies, 13 were engaged in petroleum and gas exploration and refining, and 18 were engaged in metal processing. In 2004, the average net profit increase of the iron and steel industry comprised a 49% rise from the previous year (Fortune China, 2004). These figures suggest that companies in the resources sector have developed relatively more quickly than companies from other sectors in the top 100 list; this was partly due to the considerable increase in demand for natural resources and raw and semi-raw materials, as a result of China's economic boom of recent years. For the current analysis, ten resources companies were selected from these 35 companies; these ten companies are listed in Table 1.2.

Six of these ten companies were also in the list of top 150 best performing Asian companies published by *Business Week* on October 24, 2005. The names of these six companies and their rankings are set out in Table 1.3.

Table 1.2 Ten Leading Listed Resources Companies in China Selected for this Study

Ranking*	Company name	Industry
1	China Petroleum & Chemical Corporation (Sinopec)	Petroleum
2	PetroChina Company Limited	Petroleum
8	Minmetals Development Co., Ltd.	Metals
9	Baoshan Iron & Steel Co., Ltd.	Metals
10	CNOOC Limited	Petroleum
12	Sinopec Shanghai Petrochemical Company Limited	Petroleum
18	Aluminum Corporation of China Limited (Chalco)	Metals
29	Beijing Shougang Co., Ltd.	Metals
71	Yanzhou Coal Mining Company Limited	Mining
87	Nanjing Iron & Steel Co., Ltd.	Metals

*Note: the companies were ranked according to their revenue in 2003. Source: (Fortune China 2004).

Table 1.3 Companies That Are Among the Top 150 Best Performing Asian Companies

Ranking	Company name
2	PetroChina
17	CNOOC (HK)
22	China Petroleum & Chemical
30	Chalco
45	Sinopec Shanghai Petrochemical
71	Yanzhou Coal Mining

Source: Business Week 2005, The best Asian performers, October 24, p.55.

Most of these ten leading companies also fell into the categories described as "national champions" (Nolan, 2001), which refers to firms that are seen to be of national interest and are also leaders in their particular industry; this has been emphasized by the government policy of building large enterprises since the 1980s (Nolan, 2001).

The growth of these resources sector firms in the metal, petroleum and gas, and mining industries also suggests that they are becoming increasingly important in the Chinese economy. Interestingly, the two companies that are used here to compare with the Chinese companies, BHP Billiton and Rio Tinto, were also among a list of Global 100 National Champions published by *The Diplomat* in 2007 (Hartcher, 2007).

The integration of the world economy and a decrease in the importance of national boundaries in the development of trade has added to the urgency of understanding these Chinese resources companies. This is especially as these companies continue to expand at an enormous speed both domestically and internationally, and aggressively seek to gain control of natural resources globally on behalf of the Chinese government. We are also increasingly seeing examples of growth strategies by these companies reflected in the news headlines; notable examples have included the failed takeover of Unocal by CNOOC (sparking national security concerns globally especially among developed countries) and the acquisition of a 12% stake in Rio Tinto jointly by the Aluminum Corporation of China and the U.S. aluminum producer Alcoa (Tan, 2008) and the takeover of Midwest Corp., a Perth-based iron ore miner, by Sinosteel Corp., one of China's largest steel makers (Tan, 2008).

THE HISTORICAL DEVELOPMENT OF LISTED COMPANIES IN CHINA

In order to gain a better understanding of leading Chinese resources companies, it is important to understand the overall context of how listed companies have developed in China and the role of government in this development. It is widely understood that the stock market has been used by the Chinese government as a tool to reform its state-owned enterprises (SOEs) (Green, 2004); this will be further discussed in Chapter 2.

After the People's Republic of China (PRC) was founded in 1949, the new government led by the Chinese Communist Party (CCP) started to rebuild the economy following the socialist model of the Soviet Union; under this model economic activities were required to follow government central planning rather than market forces (Wei, 2003: 91). Major enterprises were also managed as administrative departments of the government rather than as stand-alone economic entities (Schipani and Liu, 2002: 7).

During nearly three decades from 1949 to 1976, China had experienced political turmoil and slow economic growth. The two well-known strategies relied upon by the government at that time were known as "The Great Leap-Forward" (1958–1960) and "The Cultural Revolution" (1966–1976). The Great Leap-Forward promoted the substitution of capital by labor and the substitution of expertise and skilled labor by enthusiasm (Goodman, 1994: 60), while Mao's Cultural Revolution was mainly aimed at attacking his rivals in the party (Goodman, 1994). Under this system, enterprises and economic development in China remained stagnant prior to 1978; this included China's resources sector firms.

Following the death of Mao Zedong, China under the leadership of Deng Xiaoping has undergone massive economic and enterprise reform since 1978. To further improve the competitiveness of SOEs, a new policy of 'grasp(ing) the large, let(ting) go of the small (*zhuada fangxiao*)' was adopted by the government (Nolan, 2001: 16) in the early 1990s; this was aimed at building up large enterprises as 'national champions' to compete with large firms in rich countries (Nolan, 2001: 17). These national champions were not only given priority access to resources, by the end of 1990s, almost all of these national champions were also listed on the stock market (Nolan, 2001: 19) to allow them to have better access to capital.

Most of the resources sector firms are on the list of national champions; this is especially the case with Sinopec, PetroChina, CNOOC, Baoshan Iron & Steel and Beijing Shougang. In terms of Sinopec, PetroChina and CNOOC, the government has also undertaken considerable restructuring at the industry level as well as at the firm level, with an aim of building internationally competitive integrated oil companies. So far, given the growing status of these firms around the world, this policy seems successful. Further analysis of this will be provided in the case study of Sinopec in Chapter 6.

Despite almost all national champions being listed on the stock market, in order to retain government control, the share ownership structures of most listed companies were so constructed that only a small number of shares were listed in the stock market as tradable shares while the majority of shares remained firmly controlled by the government as non-tradable shares. This was the prevailing pattern before the split structure reform was carried out in 2005.

THE SPLIT SHARE OWNERSHIP STRUCTURE REFORM AND CORPORATE GOVERNANCE

The split share ownership structure refers to the fact that in most listed companies in China, only a small percentage of shares (usually below 50%) are listed and tradable on the stock market. The majority of shares (usually more than 50%) are held by a government or quasi-government entity as non-tradable shares (which are not tradable on the stock market) and can only be traded between Chinese legal persons[1] with the approval of the government.

The split share ownership structure is a by-product of China's gradualist approach to its economic and enterprise reform and it was used as a tool to maintain state ownership (with the government holding majority non-tradable shares); it also allowed the sale of some shares to the market to help to revive the then ailing SOEs by raising more capital in the stock market (Lee, 2008).

China's gradualist approach to economic and enterprise reform was regarded as a more favorable strategy over the so-called 'shock therapy' approach adopted by most former Eastern European socialist countries. However, with the progress of these reforms, the residual effect of this gradualist approach (the split share ownership structure) became an impediment to further development of China's stock market.

The Chinese government was well aware of the split share structure problem and its negative effect on disciplining listed companies through the market mechanism, and it had been planning to reform the split share ownership structure for some time. However, market sentiment has always been negative towards this reform. Any news on the split ownership structure reform would bring a new round of stock price falls, as majority ownership by the government was viewed as providing an assurance, (i.e., in case of stock market crash) that the government will always bail out the market. Without this government support, the stock market was often deemed by the general public as being too risky to invest in.[2]

Despite negative market sentiment toward the split structure reforms, the PRC government was determined to undertake the reform to eliminate this structural flaw in China's stock market. Well aware of market and popular sentiments, the government started planning to introduce this reform gradually. On January 31, 2004, the State Council issued an official document entitled 'State Council's opinions on further reforming and maintaining the stability of the capital market' (*guowuyuan guanyu tuijin ziben shichang gaige kaifang he wending fazhan de ruogan yijian*) (The State Council of China, 2004), hereinafter referred to as 'Opinions'. In the Opinions, apart from emphasizing general issues related to further development of the stock market, the split share ownership structural problem was also raised as one of the major concerns:

> The split share ownership structure problem shall be dealt with properly. The conversion of non-tradable shares to tradable shares in listed companies shall be regulated to prevent the loss of state assets in the process. The problems of non-tradable shares in listed companies shall be dealt with gradually in light of the rules of the market, i.e. the non-tradable shares shall be dealt with in a way not only to benefit the market but also to help to ensure that the interests of minority shareholders are protected.[3] (The State Council of China, 2004: 4)

Following the guidance of the Opinions and after more than a year of planning, on May 9, 2005, the first four firms would experiment with the reform of converting non-tradable shares into tradable shares (People's Daily Online, 2005c). On June 19, 2005, another 42 firms were named for inclusion in the second round of this experiment (People's Daily Online, 2005b). By the end of 2005, more than 400 firms had initiated reform to their split share ownership structure; among them, 222 firms had finished their reforms (Ren, 2005). To make all shares of a listed company tradable, a typical split share structure reform plan normally involved offering additional shares or funds to public investors as a compensation (People's Daily Online, 2005a); this is to ensure that minority-shareholders' interests are protected.

In August 2005, the China Securities and Regulatory Commission (CSRC), the State-owned Assets Supervision and Administration Commission (SASAC), the Ministry of Finance, the People's Bank of China and the Ministry of Commerce (CSRC et al., 2005) jointly issued another important policy document: 'Guidance on split share structure reform in listed companies' (*guanyu shangshi gongsi guquan fenzhi gaige de zhidao yijian*), hereinafter referred to as 'Guidance'. The Guidance sought to provide further policy advice on reforming the split share ownership structure following the Opinions issued by the State Council in January 2004. It was also specifically stipulated in the Guidance that the reform did not aim to dilute the ownership of the government, but rather to give the shares owned by the government the same rights and responsibilities as the tradable shares held by the general public—the minority shareholders. By making them potentially tradable, the shares owned by the government would also be subject to market discipline.

By giving the same tradable rights to the previously non-tradable shares owned by the government, the government could also choose to increase its shares through the market if necessary. As stated in the Guidance:

> The split share ownership structure reform is to make policy arrangements to allow non-tradable shares to be converted into tradable shares (to make sure that the shares held by the government have the same rights and responsibilities as tradable shares); the aim of the reform is *not* to sell-off the shares owned by the government to the market. At the current development stage, the government does not plan to sell-off state-owned shares to raise capital. Once the non-tradable shares become tradable, the controlling shareholder will have more flexibility to adjust its share ownership structure in order to follow the overall strategic reform of the whole country.[4] (CSRC et al., 2005: 2)

In the Guidance, it was further stated that:

> In strategic industries while government controlled listed companies are playing crucial roles in supporting the national economy, the government should maintain its controlling status and its influence on the overall development of the economy. In those strategic industries,

government should also increase its shareholdings through the stock market if necessary.[5] (CSRC et al., 2005: 3)

To further guide these split share structure reforms, the CSRC issued another document entitled: 'Administrative measures on the split share structure reform of listed companies' (*shangshi gongsi guquan fenzhi gaige guanli banfa*), hereinafter referred to as 'Administrative Measures'. The Administrative Measures specified the operational issues that related to the split share structure reform, especially the measures seeking to maintain fair treatment of minority shareholders in the process of the reform, as stated in Article 16 of these measures which states:

> Article 16   The reform plan of a listed company shall be approved by shareholders who own at least two-thirds of voting shares at a shareholders' meeting. Such reform plan shall also be approved by shareholders who own at least *two-thirds of tradable voting shares* at the shareholders' meeting. (CSRC, 2005: 4)

The Administrative Measures also stipulated that non-tradable shareholders were required to give specific guarantees to ensure that minority-shareholders' interests were properly protected in the process, as stated in Articles 23 and 24:

> Article 23   Non-tradable shareholders of a listed company shall provide guarantees following the requirement of the stock exchanges and securities depository and clearing company. The non-tradable shareholders shall provide guarantees by issuing a statement in writing indicating that they will faithfully perform their obligation as stipulated in the guarantees.

> Article 24   The non-tradable shareholders cannot transfer their shares before their guarantees are fully performed unless the parties acquiring the shares agree and are capable of fulfilling the guarantees for the non-tradable shareholders.[6] (CSRC, 2005: 6–7)

The sell-off by companies of these non-tradable shares to the market should also follow the rules as stipulated in the Administrative Measures, as stated in Article 27:

> Article 27   The sale of non-tradable shares shall comply with the following provisions:

> (1) The non-tradable shares shall not be traded or transferred within 12 months from the date of implementation of the split share structure reform plan;

(2) Upon expiry of the lock-up period as stated in Article 27.1 of the Measures, a non-tradable shareholder who holds more than 5% of the total shares of a listed company, may sell up to 5% of the total shares of the company in 12 months and up to 10% of the total shares in 24 months. The shares should be sold in the open market of the stock exchange. (CSRC, 2005: 7)

The overview of the reform plan suggested that the government was also taking a gradualist approach to its split share ownership structure reforms, which is consistent with the approach taken by the government in the overall economic and enterprise reform effort in China.

Three years after the commencement of the split share structure reforms, most listed companies had eliminated the split share ownership structure and the shares owned by the government are now also tradable on the stock market.[7] Although a major aim of the split share ownership structure reforms was to convert the non-tradable shares into tradable shares, the stock market has dipped to a two-year low recently due to concerns that there was a lack of transparency in releasing non-tradable shares to the market as tradable shares (Yi, 2008).

Furthermore, it has been suggested that less prudent procedures in issuing new shares to the market will also damage the overall development of the stock market in China (Yi, 2008). Despite the current market uncertainty, and the likelihood that the government will sell off more shares to foreign and corporate shareholders in the split share structure reform process (Lee, 2008), the government's control of a majority of shares in leading resources companies will remain relatively stable as these companies are seen as being of strategic importance to the further economic development of China.

THE IMPORTANCE OF UNDERSTANDING CORPORATE GOVERNANCE IN RESOURCES COMPANIES IN CHINA

The unique ownership structure of listed companies in China illustrates that research into corporate governance in China should be studied under its unique circumstances. Furthermore, the relatively short history of the Chinese stock market and the weak enforcement of the law through its legal system suggest that establishing a good corporate governance system remains a long-term challenge for the Chinese government. Recently, as China's domestic A-share[8] market fell 40% from its peak level, the effectiveness of its governance system was raised again, especially in terms of the poor level of corporate transparency and the lack of protection provided for minority shareholders (Newell, 2008).

Despite the growing importance of Chinese resources companies in the world economy, their corporate governance practices and mechanisms have remained less well understood by the outside world. In later chapters, we explore this theme by providing a detailed analysis of corporate governance practices in these leading resources companies in China and compare their practices with those of some of the world's leading resources companies.

2 The Regulatory Environment of Listed Companies in China

AN OVERVIEW OF GOVERNMENT POLICIES AND CORPORATE GOVERNANCE ISSUES

Despite the rapid development of leading Chinese resources companies and their growing "known" status around the world in the past few years, their corporate governance structures and practices remain less well known to the outside world. It is also understood that the stock market in China has mainly been used as a tool to revitalize China's state-owned enterprises (SOEs) on the one hand, and on the other to maintain government control of listed companies (Green, 2004: 66). Before the split share structure reform was carried out in 2005, the majority of shares were still held by the government as non-tradable shares and the government was still in de facto control of most listed companies, including resources companies.

The control of listed companies by the government in effect meant that listed companies in China were still treated as part of the administrative hierarchy of the government. As such, China was often criticized for adopting a too "legalistic approach" in managing the corporate governance of its listed companies.

Chen (1994) has observed that ad hoc administrative measures have been used by the government in authorizing the provision of economic rights to various agents; this applied especially to the rights to operate SOEs or quasi-SOEs. Strong evidence of the government of China taking a strong hand in market regulation and intervening by using administrative measures was also recently re-examined by Brahm (2003). For example, economic development in China since 1953—four years after the People's Republic of China was founded—was mainly guided by the government's five-year plans, and these were followed even after the open door policy was adopted in 1978.

Apart from the period 1949–1952, which was categorized as the economic recovery period, and the period 1963–1965, the adjustment period for the national economy (State-owned Assets Supervision and Administration Commission of the State Council, 2004), economic development in China since 1949 was mainly directed by the government's five-year plans. Among them, the sixth five-year plan (1981–1985) was the first five-year plan formulated after China adopted its open door policy in 1978; and it was not until the ninth five-year plan (1996–2000) that the "establishment of modern enterprises system and a socialist market economy" was raised as one of the important tasks.

In the tenth five-year plan (2001–2005), it was further emphasized that the establishment of an effective corporate governance system is also one of the important tasks in establishing the modern enterprise system. Various questions related to corporate governance were raised during drafting of the tenth five-year plan, and experts claimed that the effective resolution of the following issues was crucial to the success of the next stage of economic and enterprise reform in China. These questions are quoted as follows:

> How to evaluate entrepreneurship? How to establish an effective in-centive system for entrepreneurs and how to transform the previous administrative management system of managers by the party to the internal corporate governance system? (Anonymous 1)

> How to protect the interest of minority shareholders; how to increase the shareholder value for majority shareholders and at the same time also protect the interest of minority shareholders? (Anonymous 2)

The focus on establishment of an effective corporate governance system in China (as stated in the government's five-year plan) highlighted the aware-ness of the importance of corporate governance among top Chinese govern-ment officials; this should not be a surprise to those who really understand China and its reformers. As stated by the former premier Zhu Rongji, "[The] market should play a major role, with corporate governance under the law taking a stronger, firmer position" (Brahm, 2003: 73).

The recognition of corporate governance issues in the government's tenth five-year plan also influenced the supervision of listed companies by the China Securities Regulatory Commission (CSRC) and the stock exchanges. The CSRC, for example, issued a *Code of Corporate Governance for Listed Companies in China* in January 2002 (China Securities and Regulatory Com-mission, 2002). The CSRC also revised its disclosure requirements for listed companies in their annual reports, semi-annual reports and quarterly reports, and its aim was to continuously improve the quality of information disclo-sure of listed companies with the ultimate goal being to improve corporate governance.

In the eleventh five-year plan (2006–2010), it was further emphasised that environmental protection and energy efficiency should also be listed as priorities to maintain long-term economic development in China (Xinhua News Agency, 2008). This is especially relevant to resources companies as the extractive nature of these companies has linked them to high envi-ronmental risk, which has posed further challenges for these companies to improve their environmental protection practices (also part of the broader stakeholder approach to corporate governance).

REGULATORY AND ADMINISTRATIVE FORCES THAT GOVERN LISTED COMPANIES THAT WERE FORMER SOES

To help us understand corporate governance practices in leading Chinese resources companies, the overall regulatory environment for listed companies in China needs to be reviewed.

Overview

Generally, listed companies in China are at least subject to four sets of regulations, as illustrated in Figure 2.1.

According to Figure 2.1, listed companies in China are not only governed by the Company Law and the Securities Law, they should also follow the rules and regulations issued by the CSRC and must comply with the Stock Exchange Listing Rules. Here, we will mainly discuss the requirements of the corporate governance code issued by the CSRC, as it is the major body of rules that is closely related to corporate governance of listed companies in China. Legislation, such as the Company Law, the Securities Law, as well as the Stock Exchange Listing Rules, also plays a role in corporate governance. However, because of weak legal enforcement in China and the strong administrative power of the government, the role of the more formal bodies of law in corporate governance in China has been rather limited; therefore, the role of legislation and its relevance to corporate governance of listed companies in China is only briefly mentioned in various chapters where appropriate.

As explained previously, in China's case, the stock market was developed mainly as a tool to revitalize inefficient and less competitive SOEs; for this reason, those publicly listed companies that are transformed SOEs had to deal with a more complicated regulatory and administrative structure.

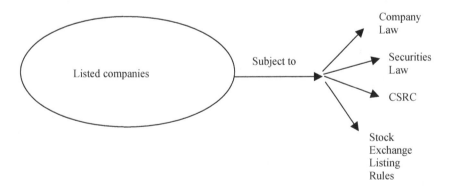

Figure 2.1   The regulatory environment for publicly listed companies in China.

Currently, the CSRC is the main regulatory organ responsible for the corporate governance of listed companies; this commission is directly under the supervision of the State Council. Previously, some listed companies were also directly or indirectly subject to the administration of different ministries through their holding company (normally an SOE).

After 1998, the supervision of those holding companies was transferred to the State Economic and Trade Commission (SETC) of the State Council; this decision was made in the First Session of the Ninth National Committee of the Chinese People's Political Consultative Conference (CPPCC) (State Economic and Trade Commission). In 2003, supervision of those holding companies was further transferred from the SETC to the State-owned Assets Supervision and Administration Commission of the State Council (SASAC). SASAC was set up to replace SETC, according to the proceedings of the Third Plenary Meeting of the First Session of the Tenth National Committee of the CPPCC.

Under such a complicated administrative structure, corporate governance is inevitably intertwined with public sector governance.[1] Therefore, administrative measures issued by the government are also reviewed in this chapter to gain a better picture of the regulatory and quasi-regulatory environment of corporate governance that applies to publicly listed companies in China.

The CSRC and the Shanghai and Shenzhen Stock Exchanges

The two mainland stock exchanges in China—the Shanghai and Shenzhen Stock Exchanges—were established in 1990 and 1991, respectively. For current purposes, we will not discuss the Hong Kong Stock Exchange here. China's principal regulator of corporate governance, the CSRC, was established in 1992 as the watchdog of China's securities and futures industries (China Knowledge Press, 2005: 198). Compared with the roles played by corresponding regulatory organs in other countries, such as with the Securities and Exchange Commission (SEC) in the US, the CSRC's power is almost unchallengeable. Both the Shanghai Stock Exchange and the Shenzhen Stock Exchange are closely regulated by the CSRC (Tomasic and Fu, 1999; Green, 2004); on the other hand, the SEC in the US is more like a monitoring organ that only has oversight over New York Stock Exchanges (Green, 2004), with the individual US states regulating particular companies.

The relationships between the CSRC and the Shanghai and Shenzhen Stock Exchanges have been somewhat unusual. Before 1997, stock exchanges were very powerful in terms of "the ability to authorize listing, regulatory responsibilities in the secondary market, the ability to discipline members, and some autonomy in policy development" (Green, 2004: 103), while the CSRC was almost excluded from the picture. However, all this changed after 1997. The CSRC assumed greater control of regulating listed companies, and the two stock exchanges became subdivisions of the CSRC following the then Premier Zhu Rongji's determination to regulate the market through direct control of the central government (Chen, 2004).

The CSRC's de jure central position in the regulation of the Chinese securities market was officially established after the new Securities Law of China came into effect on July 1, 1999 (Tomasic and Fu, 1999). The CSRC also enjoys the power of formulating policies, supervising equity listings and monitoring information disclosure, supervising the securities market and listed companies (China Online, 2000). In January 2002, the CSRC also issued a *Code of Corporate Governance for Listed Companies in China* (The Code) to further regulate listed companies in the area of corporate governance. The CSRC's position was further strengthened after the passage of the new Company Law in 2005, with CSRC's approval essential for new listing or issuance of new shares by a listed company (People's Republic of China, 2005). In addition, directors' roles and responsibilities have since been formally recognized and further strengthened since the publication of the 2005 Company Law.

Other Administrative Forces in Play

In China's case, the government has primarily played a significant role in the corporate governance of listed companies through its administrative powers. Apart from the CSRC, there are other administrative forces that play a role in the governance of listed companies in China. For example, the old system of Party and the labor union (both the party and the union are under the control of the government) is still more or less playing its role in corporate governance in those listed companies that were transformed from SOEs. The roles of the party and the union in corporate governance of listed resources companies in China is further explored in Chapter 4.

Listed companies with SOEs as dominant shareholders are still treated by the government as SOEs. In most cases, the controllers of listed companies are still party members; this is probably why the members of the State Council still believe that proper conduct and ensuring anti-corruption should be applied to party members (*dangfeng lianzheng jianshe*) and that this will help improve corporate governance in listed companies that have been transformed from SOEs. The disciplinary and administrative actions taken by the party could also alleviate the "agency problem" between the state shares and its agents—senior executives (usually appointed by the government and the party); however, the question of how best to protect the interests of minority shareholders against exploitation by the dominant shareholder remains a key concern.

REGULATORY FORCES THAT GOVERN
LISTED COMPANIES IN KEY INDUSTRIES

A key industry in China is defined as an industry that has a vital role in the development of the national economy of China, being of economic or strategic interest. Listed companies in key industries were usually formed from big SOEs and were accustomed to being under the tight control of the government, as the healthiness of those companies was seen as vital to the overall development of China. All ten listed resources companies in China discussed in this book were under the supervision of various key SOEs (which themselves were controlled by different ministries) before being listed on the stock exchanges. The ownership structure of each of those companies usually includes a dominant shareholder; in most cases, the dominant shareholder is an SOE or parent entity.

The dominant shareholder has played a very important role in corporate governance in China. At most times, the dominant shareholder is supervised by SASAC, whose responsibility is to perform as the investor on behalf of the state (Li, 2003). Major roles of SASAC include appointing and removing top executives of listed companies (which it has control of through majority ownership), evaluating the performances of those executives and granting rewards or inflicting punishments (Li, 2003). SASAC can also appoint a supervisory board in a listed company when state shares are extremely large (State-owned Assets Supervision and Administration Commission of the State Council, 2004). A simple supervisory structure of a listed company in a key industry is illustrated in Figure 2.2.

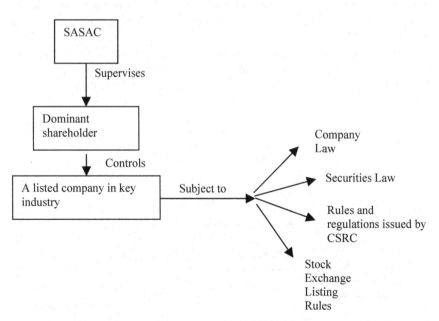

Figure 2.2   The regulatory environment of a publicly listed company that emerged from a big SOE.

Figure 2.2 illustrates that a listed company that has been created out of a big SOE is subject to government control in two ways: first, the listed company itself is at least subject to four sets of regulations, the Company Law, the Securities Law, rules and regulations issued by the CSRC and the Stock Exchange Listing Rules; second, government is heavily reliant on administrative measures to regulate listed companies (through the dominant shareholding by SOEs). For example, the CSRC is a ministerial-level department directly under the supervision of the State Council; the dominant shareholder, who is often in de facto control of the company, is also subject to the control and administration of SASAC—a *Ting*-level (one level higher than a ministerial level) department directly under the supervision of the State Council.

The governance of listed companies in key industries is further complicated by the historical development of SOEs and listed companies. Under the planned economy, economic activities such as supply, production and distribution were carried on by SOEs and companies in key industries; these were SOEs that were under the control of its corresponding ministry, which was under the control of the central government.

As indicated in Figure 2.3, before the economic and enterprise reforms carried out in China in 1978, economic activities were managed through various government departments. A department that was directly under the supervision of a government ministry was ranked as a *Si* or *Ju*, a department under a *Si* or *Ju* had a lower-level ranking and was called *Chu*. A *Si* (*Ju*)- or *Chu*-level organization could also be a SOE. After the reform in 1978, some of the *Si* (*Ju*)-level SOEs were transformed into corporations, with their subdivisions (*Chu*) being transformed into subsidiary corporations. The previous *Si Zhang* (Head of *Si*) or *Ju Zhang* (Head of *Ju*) subsequently became general managers of those newly

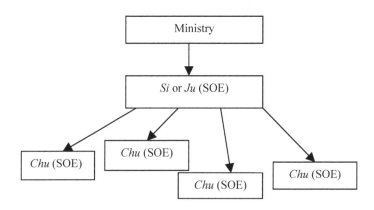

Figure 2.3   Management hierarchy of an SOE in a key industry before reform.

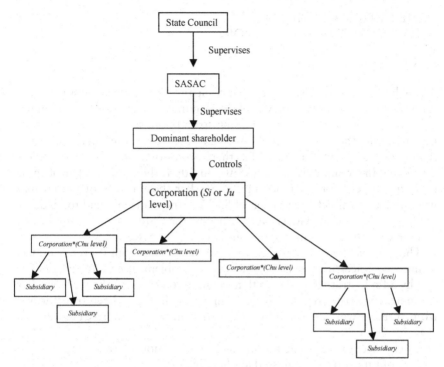

Figure 2.4 Pyramid shareholding and complicated state shareholding structures in corporate groups. *Not all of these corporations are listed.

corporatized enterprises and these general managers also kept their government rankings.

After the Shanghai and Shenzhen Stock Exchanges were established in 1990 and 1991, respectively, some of the corporatized enterprises were listed on these two stock exchanges. The typical shareholding structure of such corporatized enterprises is listed in Figure 2.4.

As is shown in Figure 2.4, the shareholding structure was in the form of a pyramid, with the dominant shareholding in listed companies (which were transformed from SOEs) controlled either by the *Si* (*Ju*)-level listed companies or by the local branches of *Si* or *Ju*. The acquisition and reorganization of related corporations also formed the basis of the origin of corporate groups in China, making the shareholding structure even more complicated.

In 1998, the abolition of 11 ministries and the establishment of three new ministries reduced the total number of ministries from 40 to 29 (Chen, 1998: B11B). At the same time, SASAC was also established to supervise state assets in key industries so as to take over the functions previously performed by the SETC.

SOME EMPIRICAL EVIDENCE OF
GOVERNMENT FORCES AT WORK

SASAC

The 'Chinese characteristics' of listed companies in China suggest that government forces will always play a role in corporate governance. In fact, Figure 2.4 only demonstrates the shareholding structure in some of the enterprises that are under the supervision of SASAC. Apart from those listed companies that were transformed from SOEs, there are also some other SOEs solely under the direct supervision of SASAC. In 2004, the total number of these two types of enterprises added up to 186. For those listed companies that were under the direct supervision of SASAC, they not only had to abide by the Code of Corporate Governance issued by the CSRC, but they also had to comply with the rules and regulations issued by SASAC.

The role that government plays in these enterprises should never be underestimated. Once the government detects a problem, it can always resolve this by administrative measures that are used to deal with the problem. For example, to further regulate listed companies that have been transformed from SOEs, it was stipulated by SASAC that in regard to these entities:[2]

1. The accounts should reflect the true situation of the company and profit must not be adjusted artificially.
2. The financial information on these companies should be fully disclosed.
3. Cost control should be strengthened in their accounting practice. Remuneration of senior management teams of these companies as well as that of their employees should strictly follow government policy. Unplanned bonuses are prohibited.
4. All income, assets, accounts receivable and payable and cash income should be fully reflected in the accounts. Keeping 'off the books' or secret accounts (*zhang wai zhang*) and 'secret money jar' (*xiao jin ku*) are prohibited.
5. Ethical practices of accounting professionals should be respected. Nobody has the right to order accounting professionals to make false financial statements.[3]

Another issue related to the governance of key listed companies is the remuneration of senior managers of those enterprises that are directly under the supervision of SASAC. The *Tentative Measures to Evaluating Performance of Senior Managers of National State-owned Enterprises*[4] *Under Direct Supervision of SASAC*, issued in late 2003, and *Tentative Measures of Remuneration of Senior Managers of National State-owned Enterprises Under Direct Supervision of SASAC*, issued in mid-2004, have illustrated from another perspective that, as both a major shareholder as well as the market regulator, the government continues to deal with corporate governance problems through administrative measures.

The Code of Corporate Governance Issued by the CSRC

Despite the intertwining of government forces with the administration of publicly listed companies, the major regulation seeking to improve the corporate governance of listed companies in China is *The Code of Corporate Governance for Listed Companies in China*, which was issued by the CSRC in January 2002.

The key areas covered in the Code correspond with other best-practice codes of corporate governance for publicly listed companies found in countries such as Australia and the Organisation for Economic Co-operation and Development (OECD) countries (Tomasic, 2005). The Code also specifically addresses the main problems associated with corporate governance in China, including the dominance of state shareholders as the main controlling shareholders in most publicly listed companies. It is necessary to further regulate the activities of controlling shareholders in order to provide better protection to all shareholders, and promote further development of the stock market. The key features of the PRC's Code are discussed below.

Chapter 1 of the Code introduces rules related to all shareholders; the regulation of "related party transactions" is specifically discussed. Proper handling of related party transactions is believed to be the key to successful separation of the activities of a listed company from its controlling shareholder. The existence of related party transactions in China is also related to the fact that some publicly listed companies belonged to corporate groups before their listing, leading to the existence of numerous business ties between them. After introducing the Code, CSRC stressed that activities with related parties must be disclosed and be well justified so as to avoid any anti-competitive practices.

Chapter 2 of the Code lays down detailed behavioral rules for controlling shareholders and their relations with listed companies. The requirements found in this chapter suggest that the Chinese government is trying to resolve the inherent problems that arise when the state is a controlling shareholder in a listed company. Another main focus of Chapter 2 is an effort to maintain the independence of a listed company; this is noted in Article 22 of the Code which states that:

A listed company shall be separated from its controlling shareholders in such aspects as personnel, assets and financial affairs, shall be independent in institution and business, shall practice independent business accounting, and shall independently bear risks and obligations. (China Securities Regulatory Commission, 2002: 5)

Chapter 3 of the Code focuses on the board of directors, and especially upon independent directors. Official regulation of independent directors commenced in 2001 with the *Guidelines for Introducing Independent Directors to the Board of Directors of Listed Companies* ("the Guideline") (China Securities Regulatory Commission, 2001) being introduced by the CSRC in September 2001. Apart from independent directors, specialized sub-committees of a company's board should also be introduced, as provided for by Article 52 of the Code:

> The board of directors of a listed company may establish a corporate strategy committee, an audit committee, a nomination committee, a remuneration and appraisal committee and other special committees in accordance with the resolutions of the shareholders' meetings. All committees shall be composed solely of directors. (China Securities Regulatory Commission, 2002: 10)

Other than the "corporate strategy committee," all other sub-committees require independent directors to serve as their chairperson.

Chapter 4 of the Code moves on to deal with supervisors and the supervisory board of a listed company. Chapter 5 focuses on "performance assessments and incentive and disciplinary systems" for management personnel and/or directors and supervisors. Chapter 6 deals with the "stakeholders" of a listed company; the recognition of stakeholders' interests is partly related to the fact that most publicly listed companies were former SOEs, which have historically remained burdened with social responsibilities to employees (Jia, 2004). Chapter 7 draws together information disclosure and transparency requirements for a listed company. Thus, Article 91 of the Code clearly sets out the requirements for information disclosure for listed companies in corporate governance, as follows:

> A listed company shall disclose information regarding its corporate governance in accordance with laws, regulations and other relevant rules, including but not limited to: (1) the members and structures of the board of directors and of the supervisory board; (2) the performance and evaluation of the board of directors and the supervisory board; (3) the performance and evaluation of the independent directors, including their attendance at board of directors' meetings, their issuance of independent opinions and their opinions regarding related party transactions and appointment and removal of directors and senior management personnel; (4) the composition and work of the specialised committees of the board of directors; (5) the actual state of corporate governance of the company, the gap between the company's corporate governance practices and the Code, and the reasons for the gap; and (6) specific plans and measures to improve corporate governance. (China Securities Regulatory Commission, 2002: 15–16)

To assist controllers of listed companies to understand the Code of Corporate Governance, as well as to implement it, the PRC government in 2002 took a number of other actions. After the CSRC issued its Code in January 2002, it announced that 2002 was to be known as "the year of improving corporate governance in publicly listed companies" (*shang shi gong si zhi li nian*). In March 2002, former Premier Zhu Rongji, in his report on the work of the government to the Fifth Plenary Session of the Ninth Chinese People's Political Consultative Conference of the People's Republic of

China (Zhu, 2002), emphasized "the need to concentrate on examining the modern corporate system established in listed companies."

In order to carry out the task of ". . .examining the modern corporate system established in listed companies" urged by Zhu (as mentioned in Zhu's report), the CSRC and the SETC issued a notice (*The notice of examination of the establishment of modern enterprise system in listed companies*) to listed companies as well as regional offices of the CSRC and the SETC so as to review the establishment of the modern enterprises system in listed companies; this followed on from the urging of the then Premier Zhu Rongji in his report to the Fifth Session of the Ninth National Committee of the Chinese People's Political Consultative Conference. Although corporate governance was not specifically mentioned in the title of the notice, the content of the notice revealed that its focus was on corporate governance issues,[5] as illustrated in the following official summary:

> Issue no. 1 deals with the 5 separations as mentioned in the Code, i.e. separation of listed companies from its controlling shareholders in personnel, financial affairs, assets, organizational structure and operations.
>
> Issue no. 2 deals with whether there is any misappropriation of listed companies' funds by its controlling shareholders.
>
> Issue no. 3 deals with whether controlling shareholders are interfering with the appointment of directors, supervisors and senior management of listed companies, and whether controlling shareholders are interfering with the decision making of listed companies.
>
> Issue no. 4: deals with the issue of related party transactions between listed companies and controlling shareholders.
>
> Issue no. 5: Enterprise reform and the positioning of enterprises.
>
> Issue no. 6: The separation of politics and enterprise management in listed companies with a dominant state holder and the current status of the reform in human resources.
>
> Issue no. 7: The functioning of the general shareholder's meeting, meetings of the board of directors and the supervisory board.
>
> Issue no. 8: The proper use of the funds raised.
>
> Issue no. 9: Information disclosure in terms of providing the interim report and the annual report.
>
> Issue no. 10: funds managed for other parties by way of commission and guarantees for other people. (Anonymous, 2002)

This notice also specified that a special meeting should be organized with company secretaries of listed companies by the regional office of the CSRC and the SETC to effectively convey these requirements. Listed companies should also self-examine the implementation of the Code. The time frame for carrying out this self-examination is listed in Table 2.1.

Table 2.1   Time Frame for the Self-examination of Corporate Governance in
Listed Companies

Time	Activities	Note
May–June 2002	Self-examination by listed companies	Result will be reported to the CSRC
July–September 2002	Examination by the regional CSRC and SETC offices of selected listed companies. CSRC will select some of these listed companies and audit them.	Model companies will be selected and their experiences will be shared with others
October–November 2002	Report produced and submitted to the CSRC	

Source: adapted from http://news.xinhuanet.com/zhengfu/2002–05/13/content_390389.htm.[6]

To support this process of self-examination, the notice was also accompanied by two other documents, respectively entitled, *"Format of self-examination report on establishing modern enterprise system in publicly listed companies"* and *"The self-examination and report format of controlling shareholders"*.

The design of the Self-examination Report was consistent with the approach taken in the CSRC's corporate governance Code and focused on compliance with the Code. The Self-examination Report has 21 pages and includes two main parts. The first part includes six sections covering the requirements of the Code, and is composed of 110 multiple choice and short-form questions. The second part comprises eight open-ended questions designed to give listed companies an opportunity to further demonstrate progress in their implementation of good corporate governance practices.

In fact, the rigidity inherent in dealing with corporate governance compliance in this way was widely criticized by controllers of listed companies.[7] One problem is that there is no flexibility in dealing with companies on a case-by-case basis. The CSRC has also lacked the resources to check listed companies on an on-going basis; the frequency of monitoring of each company has occurred only once in every two years.[8] Some people have also said that rigid regulation by the CSRC has made the operations of companies less efficient.[9]

Compliance with the Code in Selected Listed Companies

To show whether publicly listed companies have complied with the Code, and especially with the disclosure requirements of the Code, it is useful to review the nature of corporate governance disclosure as reflected in selected annual reports for publicly listed companies; these have been drawn from 2002 reports.

As the number of listed companies in China has grown steadily over the past decade it is well beyond the scope of this book to review the annual reports of all listed companies in China. However, it may be useful to look at reports from a group of firms selected from the list of China's top 100 companies published in *Fortune* magazine (Chen and Florian, 2002) in September 2002. The *Fortune* magazine list was chosen because most of these companies emerged out of SOEs and were in key industries; this group of companies was also somewhat under the control of government.

A quick examination of China's top 100 listed companies revealed that 26 companies were only listed on overseas stock exchange(s) and/or on the Hong Kong Stock Exchange,[10] while 74 companies were listed on the Shanghai or Shenzhen Stock Exchanges. Only disclosures made by these 74 companies in their 2002 annual reports[11] were examined and the key points arising from these disclosures were tabulated in order to gain an overview of their compliance with the disclosure provisions of the Code. These key points are summarized as follows.

All annual reports of the 74 companies examined here have separate sections entitled, "Corporate Governance Structure." There were also four other headings: "Top Ten Largest Shareholders," "Brief Introduction on Directors, Supervisors and Senior Management," "Brief Introduction on Shareholders' Meeting" and "Board of Supervisors' Report." All four sections of these selected companies' annual reports were examined as they were all deemed relevant to corporate governance. The corporate governance disclosures of these selected companies are summarized as follows,

> First, the Code requires companies to disclose the names of their ten largest shareholders. All 74 companies disclosed their ten largest shareholders. All except China Minsheng Bank had controlling shareholders, and most of the ten largest shareholders were SOEs, government departments and legal persons holding non-tradable shares. Recent changes in *The Rules for Information Disclosure of Publicly Listed Companies,* No. 2 Content and Format of the Annual Report, also asked listed companies to disclose their ten largest tradable-share holders and the connections, if any, that existed between them in order to further enhance the quality of information disclosure of these publicly listed companies (Lin, 2003).

The Code also requires the disclosure of corporate governance practices in general. In their 2002 annual reports, all 74 companies provided an overview of their corporate governance practices under the heading "Corporate Governance Structure." Some of the companies only briefly stated that they have complied with the Company Law, the Securities Law and the Code and followed the Self-examination Report, while others have provided more detailed disclosure, such as whether the company has set up any relevant corporate codes relating to corporate governance. Nanjing

Iron & Steel Co., Ltd. even revealed that, to strengthen its corporate governance, 19 new general management policies and 60 policies focusing on specific areas have either been revised or formulated. Most companies revised their articles of association to accommodate the new requirements set out in the Code. The most common rules and codes adopted by these 74 companies are listed as follows:

Rules for Shareholders' Meetings
Rules for Board of Directors' Meetings
Procedures for Supervisory Board Meetings
Procedure of Information Disclosure
Work Rules for Independent Directors
Rules Governing Related-Party Transactions
Work Rules for the CEO

While it is difficult to gauge the level of implementation of these corporate governance rules and practices by simply reviewing the annual reports (Chapter 4, based on interviews with government officials and controllers of resources companies, will be able to provide more insights on this), the swiftness in introducing corporate governance practices to listed companies, even only superficially, illustrated that the Chinese government played an important role in regulating listed companies through its controlling stake.

In terms of disclosures about directors, supervisors and senior management, all 74 companies disclosed the name, age, gender and tenure of their directors, supervisors and senior management. Four companies also disclosed their senior officers' biographical details. In regard to the disclosure of duties fulfilled by independent directors, a total of 61 companies disclosed information on the performance of independent directors and most of them were displayed under the heading: Performance of Independent Directors. The disclosures of most companies in regard to duties fulfilled by independent directors can be as brief as that quoted in the following two paragraphs, which were excerpted from *TCL Communication Equipment Co. Ltd.*[12] *2002 Annual Report:*[13]

According to the requirements of "Guidelines for Introducing Independent Directors to the Board of Directors of Listed Companies" and "Code of Corporate Governance for Listed Companies in China", TCL has set up Independent Director System of TCL Co. Ltd. . . (TCL Communication Equipment Corporation Limited, 2003: 12)

TCL has three independent directors, and one of them is an accounting professional. All three directors have faithfully, honestly and diligently fulfilled their duties and attended the board and the shareholders' meetings; safeguarded the company and the shareholders' interest. Acting as independent experts, independent directors have also advised the company on issues such as related party transactions and other crucial decisions. (TCL Communication Equipment Corporation Limited, 2003: 12)

The very general nature of the disclosure of the duties performed by independent directors does raise questions regarding the actual performance of independent directors. The establishment and performance of specialized committees of the board of directors was also disclosed by most companies. The Code stipulates that a corporate strategy committee, an audit committee, a nomination committee and a remuneration and appraisal committee may be established in a listed company. Among the selected 74 companies examined here, 27 companies have set up specialized committees under their board of directors. Among them, seven companies have set up all four committees. Tsingtao Brewery has also set up a corporate governance committee.

The close relationship between a listed company and its controlling shareholder (usually an SOE) often gave rise to related party transactions. To demonstrate transparency in this area, fifty-eight companies disclosed in their annual reports that their controlling shareholders were independent from the listed entities. A few companies also provided detailed accounts regarding the separation of the operations of controlling shareholders from those of the listed companies. The 2002 annual reports of most of the 74 companies examined have disclosed whether there were any related party transactions and their appropriateness. However, only a third of these companies provided a brief explanation on how the relationships with major stakeholders of the companies were managed.

Disclosure regarding the shareholders' meeting was another matter that was reviewed in the companies' annual reports. The organization of shareholders' meetings was often mentioned in a section of the annual report following the "Corporate Governance Structure" section, and a brief overview was given on the operation of the shareholders' meeting (this occurred in each of the 74 companies' 2002 annual reports). The supervisory board report was also included in all of these selected 2002 company reports.

It is worth noting that the administrative measures were carried out in a formal way by the listed companies. For example, in the 2002 annual report of Sinopec Shanghai Petrochemical Company Limited, it is stated that,

According to the *No. 9 Rules for Information Disclosure for Companies Issuing Securities* issued by the CSRC, the return on equity and earning per share is calculated as follows . . . (Sinopec Shanghai Petrochemical Company Limited, 2003: 6)

Overall, the above brief examination of the annual reports of 74 publicly listed companies demonstrates that selected companies generally complied in form with the requirements of the Code regarding corporate governance disclosure. The speedy adoption of corporate governance disclosure exemplified "the strong regulation" approach undertaken by China to improve its corporate governance in the transition period of its economic and enterprise reform (Schutt et al., 2001). It has also illustrated that the "dominant state shareholder" has played an important role in improving corporate governance disclosure in publicly listed companies. By acting as the "dominant shareholder" on the one hand and "the regulator" (CSRC) on the other, the government has had a distinct advantage in maneuvering corporate governance in publicly listed companies in China.

SUMMARY

This chapter has discussed the regulatory and quasi-regulatory environment for listed companies in China. It illustrated the unique characteristic of corporate governance in China, with government administrative measures playing an important role. A review of regulatory forces that govern listed companies in key industries is important, as all leading Chinese resources companies examined in this book belong to this category. By illustrating the government's role in promoting *The Code of Corporate Governance for Listed Companies in China* (issued by the CSRC in January 2002), it further demonstrates that government administrative measures are embedded in all aspects of the governance of listed companies in China.

3 Understanding Governance in Resources Sector Companies
Is Disclosure Adequate?

INTRODUCTION

Understanding the regulatory environment and the role of government in promoting good corporate governance practices in listed companies in China has paved the way for further development of corporate governance practices and mechanisms in leading Chinese resources companies. This chapter examines corporate governance practices (as disclosed in annual reports) of the ten leading resources companies in China and uses disclosures made by leading resources companies in Australia as a basis for comparison.

There are good reasons for using resources companies in Australia. First, in recent years we have seen further integration of the Chinese and the Australian economies. Data from the Australian Bureau of Statistics (ABS) shows that China overtook Japan and the US to become Australia's largest trading partner in 2007 (Uren, 2007); this is partly due to the increased export of natural resources to China. Secondly, the resources sector also plays a very important role in the Australian economy, as Australia is a leading resources exporting country. As proponents of the free trade agreement between China and Australia have also argued, there is considerable complementarity between these two economies (DFAT, 2008).

The resources sector in Australia is well developed and has been a major contributor to the Australian economy since the gold rush years of the 1850s (Australian Mines and Metals Association, 2001: 3; 2004: 6). This sector is not only one of the major contributors to the Australian commodity export market (Australian Mines and Metals Association, 2004), it also plays a significant role in Australia's domestic economy. For example, in 2003, the mining sector contributed 5.6% to Australian GDP (The Australasian Institute of Mining and Metallurgy, 2004). In 2003, the minerals and petroleum resources sector comprised 37% of total exports of goods and services from Australia (The Australasian Institute of Mining and Metallurgy, 2004).

There is clearly a close link between the fast growing Chinese economy and the booming mining industry in Australia. The small domestic market in Australia has never been a factor in determining the world price of mining products, and previous mining booms have often resulted from overseas mineral price rises (Salsbury and Sweeney, 1988: 345). However, in recent years, the major forces for growth came from China—one of most resource-hungry countries in the twenty-first century. As BlueScope Steel's former Managing Director and CEO, Kirby Adams, put it:

> China is extremely important to my company [BlueScope Steel] and increasingly important to our nation—Australia . . . There is every reason to believe that the 21st century may be the Chinese century. (Adams, 2004: 1)

There have already been major cooperative efforts between resources sector companies in China and in Australia; for example, a $25 billion agreement was signed in 2002 between the China National Offshore Oil Corporation (CNOOC) and Woodside Petroleum to supply liquefied natural gas to China (Callick et al., 2002). Reference can also be made to the agreement made between BHP Billiton and four Chinese steel makers (Wuhan Iron and Steel Corporation, Maanshan Iron & Steel Company, Jiangsu Shagang Iron and Steel, and Tangshan Iron & Steel Company) to jointly invest in a mine in Western Australia (Taylor and Ryan, 2005).

The operation of a free-trade agreement between Australia and China since 2005 has further boosted Chinese investment in Australian resources projects (Lewis and Armitage, 2005: 1). Recent deals have seen Aluminium Corporation of China (Chinalco) (together with Alcoa) buying a 9% stake in Rio Tinto; the $1.2 billion hostile takeover of Midwest Corporation by Sinosteel; APAC & Shougang's 40% stake (worth $1 billion) in Mount Gibson Iron (Burrell, 2008) and the purchase of controlling shares of Abra Mining by a Chinese government-controlled group—Hunan Nonferrous Metals (Vaughan, 2008). Recently, Sinosteel secured the approval to buy up to 49.9% of Murchison Metals, which is a small Perth-based mining company (Sutherland, 2008). All these factors provide a good reason for comparing the resources sector in Australia so as to guage corporate governance patterns in Chinese mining companies.

SELECTION OF RESOURCES COMPANIES IN AUSTRALIA

To enhance comparability, firms in the Australian resources sectors were chosen from the top 500 listed companies in Australia (Ng et al., 2004). Among the ten chosen resources companies, some are diversified resources companies and some have specialized in mining, petrochemical and metals. The ten selected Australian resources companies are listed in Table 3.1.

Table 3.1   Ten Listed Resources Companies in Australia Selected for this Study

Ranking*	Company
3	BHP Billiton
6	Rio Tinto
23	Woodside Petroleum
31	WMC Resources**
26	BlueScope Steel
84	OneSteel
101	Newcrest Mining
70	Minara Resources
41	Equatorial Mining
45	Alumina

*Note: the companies were ranked according to their net profit in 2003.
Source: *Business Review Weekly*, 2004, vol. 26, no. 16, pp. 64–73.
** WMC Resources has now been acquired by BHP Billiton.

Companies were selected according to their size, as corporate governance in large companies tends to be the subject of more open public debate than it is in smaller companies.

CORPORATE GOVERNANCE IN CHINA AND AUSTRALIA

Although resources companies drawn from both countries operate in similar industries, resources companies in China operate in a different regulatory and market environment from those in Australia. In Australia, there is a mature stock market and a relatively competitive market environment. However, this does not mean that Australia does not have its own corporate governance problems. The mining boom and bust of the 1960s (Sykes, 1978; Senate Select Committee on Securities and Exchange, 1974), the problematic 1980s with scandals involving so-called corporate 'cowboys' (Tomasic and Bottomley, 1993) and the more recent mega-collapse of HIH Insurance (The HIH Royal Commission, 2003), all suggest that there is still much room for improvement in terms of promoting good corporate governance in Australia.

In contrast, the relatively short history of stock market development in China has not given it a great deal of experience to draw upon; the stock markets in Shanghai and Shenzhen are relatively young compared with those in Australia, where the first stock exchange was set up in the nineteenth century; the Shanghai and Shenzhen Stock Exchanges were only established in 1990 and 1991, respectively. China's stock markets are often criticized for being relatively 'controlled' markets, as there is often heavy government interference in these mainland stock markets; this of course does not generally apply to the securities market in Hong Kong.

In China, government is not only the regulator of stock markets, it is also the biggest shareholder in many big publicly listed companies operating in key industries. Some recent statistics can demonstrate this point: by the end of 2001, the state as the ultimate shareholder controlled 81% of all listed companies in China (Liu and Sun, 2005: 48). The average controlling stake held by the largest shareholder in China's listed companies is often more than 49% (Liu and Sun, 2005: 48). Despite the share split ownership structure reforms (discussed in Chapter 1), the current governance arrangements of major listed Chinese companies (as illustrated in Chapter 2) are unlikely to change dramatically in the near future.

Before analyzing corporate governance disclosures by companies in China and Australia, the different corporate governance models used in these two countries need to be discussed. Generally, two broad market models that relate to corporate governance are to be found: the outsider-based model and the insider-based model. These are each discussed in detail in the following section.

THEORETICAL FOUNDATION—CORPORATE GOVERNANCE MODELS AROUND THE WORLD

The dominant corporate governance model found in a given country is closely related to its political, legal and economic conditions. Generally speaking, there are at least two broad types of capitalist economy, one that is more socially driven and the other that is more market driven. Two typical examples of socially driven economies are to be found in Germany and Japan, while the more market-driven approach is to be found in Anglo-American countries, such as the US and the UK. The different types of capitalism in Germany and Japan are supported by socially embedded economic institutions, and long-term commitments and mutual trust among economic agents (Streeck and Yamamura, 2003: 1). On the other hand, Anglo-American economies are dominated by market-driven transactions focused mainly on short-term gains (Streeck and Yamamura, 2003: 1). In Anglo-American–style market-driven economies, outsiders are more effective in controlling ownership relations within listed companies through their capacity to take control of shares through stock market trading. In constrast, in more socially driven economies, the ready transferability of shares on stock markets is more restricted by the role of block holding institutions such as banks and financial institutions.

Thus, associated with the two broad types of capitalism referred to above, the structure of corporate ownership and control has often been categorized into two major types: the outsider-based system and the insider-based system (Mayer, 1994: 189). Accordingly, the corporate governance models associated with different ownership structures are often called the outsider-based model and the insider-based model. The simple forms of ownership structure in these two systems are illustrated in Figure 3.1.

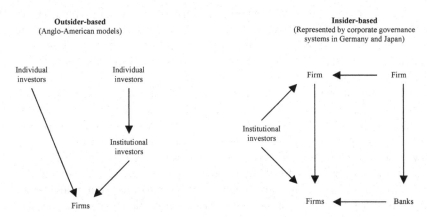

Figure 3.1 Ownership structures in the two main corporate governance models. Source: (Mayer, 1994).

A typical ownership structure found in the outsider-based model can be as simple as that illustrated in Figure 3.1. Both individual and institutional investors could become shareholders of firms; individual investors could also invest in firms that could be categorized as institutional investors for other firms. However, the ownership structure in the insider-based model is more complex, as in such models there is often an interlocking of ownership among firms, banks and other institutional investors, as shown on the right-hand side of Figure 3.1. Outsider-based models are often to be found in countries that are more oriented toward market economies and have less government intervention; in contrast, the insider-based model is more often found in countries where social values are historically more embedded when compared with economic values. To further understand the major characteristics of outsider-based and insider-based models, their representatives, the Anglo-American, and the German and Japanese corporate governance models, are briefly examined in the following sections. This is important as China has drawn upon elements of each model as it has built its evolving systems of corporate governance.

The Outsider-based Model—Ownership Structure in the US and the UK

The outsider-based model is sometimes called the "Anglo-American model" or the "UK–US model." In fact, there remain stark differences in corporate governance practices in the US and the UK, but we can ignore these for present purposes. Overall, the major characteristics of the so-called Anglo-American model include dispersed–shareholder ownership and a liquid capital market where ownership and control rights are frequently traded (Franks and Mayer quoted by Stapledon, 1996b: 3). The corporate governance model found in Australia is generally believed to be a subset of the Anglo-American model (Cheffins, 2002a). It is also said that in the 1990s China started to adopt some of the features of the Anglo-American model (Tam, 1999: 24), although China's underlying market structure is closer to the Japanese model.

Ownership structures in the UK and the US have been characterized by dispersed–share ownership as described by Berle and Means in their conception of the modern corporation (Berle and Means, 1932). Normally small shareholders only holds a relatively small parcel of shares, so that if they have concerns about governance issues, it is easier for them to simply 'vote with their feet' (and sell their shares) than to actively participate in exercising their ownership rights (such as by monitoring the management). This is because a simple cost–benefit analysis shows that to exercise owner-ship rights, one has to incur the total cost for only a pro rata share of the gains, if any (Monks and Minow, 2001: 110). In other words, there are high costs and many free riders when one shareholder takes action to try to correct problems in the company's governance.

Furthermore, the liquid share markets that exists in the UK and the US, make it relatively easy for shareholders to diversify, and have made share-holders even more passive in exercising their ownership rights. These fac-tors have rendered de facto control of the company to management, hence creating the root of the so-called agency problem (Jensen and Meckling, 1976). Agency problems occur when management acting as the agent of the principal (shareholders) pursues their own self-interests rather than acting in the best interests of their shareholders. Although there has been a rise in the number of institutional investors[1] in the US and the UK, they have for historical reasons preferred to play a passive role in corporate governance matters (Roe, 1994); this has largely left the features associated with the dispersed-ownership structure unchanged.

The Outsider-based Model—Corporate Governance Models in the US and the UK

The corporate governance model of a typical publicly listed company oper-ating in the US and the UK is illustrated in Figure 3.2.

As demonstrated in this figure, the UK–US type of corporate governance model (a version of which is also found in Australia) is composed of inter-nal and external mechanisms. As illustrated in the internal mechanism on the left-hand side of Figure 3.2, shareholders appoint a board of directors who then appoint and monitor managers; and at the same time managers operate the core functions of the corporation and report back to the board of directors, who represent shareholders. It is also worth noting that there is only a one-tier board in the UK–US corporate governance model. The one-tier board is often composed of executive directors and non-executive directors or outside directors depending on whether it is in the US or the

Internal   **External**

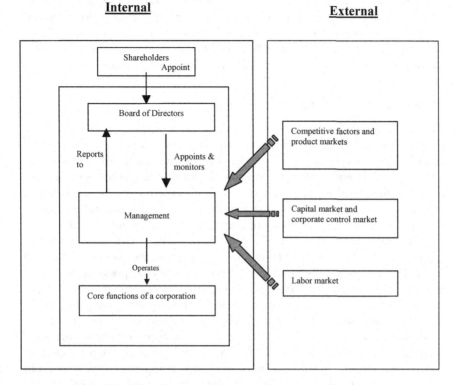

Figure 3.2 Dominant corporate governance models in the UK and the US. Source: adapted from World Bank (World Bank, 2003), (Broadman, 2001).

UK, and the number of the board members will vary according to the regulations and practices in their respective countries.

The right-hand side of Figure 3.2 shows that external market forces, such as competitive factors in the product market, capital market, corporate control market and the labor market, in theory act as further monitoring mechanisms for achieving management accountability. Competitive factors in the product market play an important monitoring role as the company's performance vis-à-vis its competitors illustrates whether managers are competent and hard-working. In addition, it is often suggested that competitive forces in the market for corporate control will expose an under-performing firm to a takeover which could lead to the ejection of its management by the acquirer (Manne, 1965). However, the threat to management from a takeover is probably less than this theory implies. Competitiveness in the labor market, especially in the executive recruitment market, can also play an important role, as it will be harder for a shirking or incompetent manager to go through the shrewd head-hunters' scrutiny to secure another job.

That is at least the theory; in reality managers exercise much more control in the US and the UK than this model suggests, as they are able to withstand efforts by dispersed shareholders to discipline or remove them. The collapse of companies such as Enron and World Com illustrate some of these failures of the outsider-based model (Armour and McCahery, 2006).

Overview of the Insider-based Model

The relevance of the insider-based model for our purposes is that the ownership structure in listed companies in China has reflected the characteristics of large block holding and insider control. In most listed companies in China, government is often the dominant shareholder, holding more than 50% of shares. China also shares a major characteristic of the German model (a subset of the insider-based model), as a listed company is required to establish a supervisory board in addition to a management board.

Corporate governance models in Germany and Japan have distinctive features that separate them from the Anglo-American model. These two broad models have influenced much contemporary corporate governance research. Corporate governance in these two countries has attracted the interest of academics following their remarkable economic performance in the late 1980s and early 1990s (Cheffins, 2002a). Corporate governance models are often determined by the structure of their respective corporate sectors, and the corporate sectors found in Germany and Japan are characterized by a relatively small number of quoted companies, and an illiquid stock market in which ownership and control rights are infrequently traded (Stapledon, 1996b: 3). Although, both countries are said to be examples of the insider-based model, corporate governance systems in Germany and Japan are discussed separately, as there are also differences between them in regard to the nature and level of involvement of different insiders.

The Insider-based Model—Corporate Governance Model in Germany

The major characteristics of the corporate governance model found in Germany include the two-tier board and the co-determination systems (du Plessis et al., 2007). Apart from a management board, a publicly listed company in Germany is also required by law to have a supervisory board. Big publicly listed companies (known as the AG or *Aktiengesellschaft*) are required by law to have employees and union representatives participating actively in corporate governance on the supervisory board (Charkham, 1995). The election of employee and union representatives to the supervisory board to join shareholder representatives is the so-called system of "co-determination"; this model is also clearly stipulated in legislation (Co-determination Act 1976). The existence of a co-determination system in Germany is closely related to the general perception of the role of corporations in German society. Generally speaking, it is said that the culture of German corporations is more co-operative and community-oriented than that of companies in the US and the UK (Charkham, 1995).

For legal and historical reasons, banks play an important role in the corporate governance of listed companies in Germany, although German banks themselves are usually not the largest shareholders in such a company (Franks and Mayer, 1997). However, as holders of the bearer shares owned by their customers, German banks are able to exercise proxy votes on behalf of dispersed shareholders (Franks and Mayer, 1997: 283). The underdevelopment of the financial market during Germany's earlier industrialization resulted in companies relying more heavily on debt financing from banks (Charkham, 1995) than on shareholder funds, as would be the case in the UK and the US. Over the years, German banks became shareholders when the companies that they lent money to could not repay their debts and had little else to offer their creditors other than their own shares (Charkham, 1995). As outlined below, this system was also made possible due to legal and historical circumstances, such as the fact that:

- The practice of banks being shareholders in a company was not precluded by law in Germany (Roe, 1994), and
- As long-term relational-type of credit providers of the company, banks understood the type of business and the industry of the company, and therefore, were well-prepared to become its shareholders (Charkham, 1995).

Apart from the bank's own shareholdings, at most times, banks were also acting as proxies for private shareholders due to the fact that German shares are mainly held in the form of bearer shares and German shareholders generally lodge these securities with their banks (Charkham, 1995: 38). This has effectively transferred the de facto voting rights of private shareholders to the banks.

The board structure of the German type of two-tier board is illustrated in the Figure 3.3.

As illustrated in Figure 3.3, the two-tier board is composed of a management board (*Vorstand*) and a supervisory board (*Aufsichtsrat*). The management board is appointed by the supervisory board (Proctor and Miles, 2002) rather than by shareholders, as is the case in the UK and the US. Additionally, the management board runs the company and its powers and duties are derived, in the main, from statute (Proctor and Miles, 2002). The average size of the German management board is about five to seven members (Theisen, 1998: 261).

Figure 3.3 also shows that the supervisory board is the main internal monitoring body within the company (Theisen, 1998) and that it has a more complex composition. The supervisory directors are often appointed by shareholders (usually banks) and employees depending on the type of

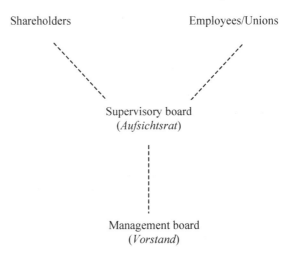

Shareholders   Employees/Unions

Supervisory board
(*Aufsichtsrat*)

Management board
(*Vorstand*)

Figure 3.3   Board structure in German companies.
Source: adapted from (Charkham,1995: 18).

company. After World War II, it became mandatory to include employee representatives on company supervisory boards in the iron, coal and steel industries (Proctor and Miles, 2002). According to the German Co-determination Act 1976, employee representatives were appointed by employees (Proctor and Miles, 2002), and by and large, employee representatives usually were trade union members (Hopt, 1998). Co-determination effectively gives employee representatives the right to participate in supervising the management board on behalf of employees. The legal size of supervisory boards depends on the number of employees within a corporation, usually comprising between 12 and 20 members (Theisen, 1998: 261). According to Hopt (1998), the supervisory board is also a relationship board as it remains a 'convenient tool' for the company to institutionalize its network, originating historically from companies' relationship-building efforts with its banks.

The Insider-based Model—Corporate Governance Model in Japan

The corporate governance model found in Japan represents a different version of the insider-based model. Before 1997, the Japanese model was also broadly followed by China (Brahm, 2003), as Chinese company-law reformers have been much influenced by Japanese legal reforms. It was argued that post-war Japan represented a type of non-liberal capitalism embedded in, and managed through, national institutions supported by a strong nation-state. It was also widely believed that in Japan political-economic and social institutions were superior to market forces in promoting long-term economic performance (Streeck and Yamamura, 2003: 5). As a consequence, successive Japanese governments fostered the growth of manufacturing industry and encouraged sub-contracting relationships between corporations. The family-oriented corporate culture in Japan (Charkham, 1995) also encouraged life-long employment and a seniority-based wage system. The existence of corporate groups in the corporate sector, with a 'main bank' providing finance to all corporations in the same group, also reinforced this family-oriented culture.

The Japanese corporate sector is characterized by the existence of powerful corporate groups (Charkham, 1995) and control-oriented shareholders (Hoshi, 1998). The management monitoring function is performed by creditors, especially the 'main bank' (Hoshi, 1998: 861). In contrast to Germany, Japanese workers do not have formal representation on a company's supervisory board (Hoshi, 1998: 861), but employees are still treated as important stakeholders of the company.

In Japan, the joint stock company is called the *kabushiki kaisha*, which is equivalent to a publicly listed company in the UK and the US (Proctor and Miles, 2002). In listed companies in Japan, banks own about 22% of total shares compared with less than 5% in the US.[2] Other than banks, individuals in Japan own about 24% of total shares, non-financial companies own about 24% and life insurance companies own about 11% (Kanda, 1998: 928).

The ownership structure of listed companies in Japan is characterized by stable shareholdings or cross-shareholding of related corporations (Okabe, 2002: 4) and by employee share ownership. Stable shareholdings indicate that there is infrequent share trading and that shareholders are more likely to focus on the long-term prospects of the company. These stable shareholders may be the company's suppliers of goods and services, creditors or customers (Proctor and Miles, 2002: 110). Statistical data also shows that major types of cross-shareholding arise where financial institutions hold the shares of business corporations and where business corporations in return hold the shares of financial institutions (Okabe, 2002: 18). This enhances the importance of the main bank system. There are also historical reasons for the existence of cross-shareholdings. These can be traced back to the late 1960s when the government amended the Commercial Law to facilitate mutual shareholding in order to prevent hostile takeovers from foreign investors (Okabe, 2002: 4).

The Employee Stock Ownership Program (ESOP) has become a very important feature of the Japanese share ownership structure. Employment in Japan is often characterized by life-long employment (Streeck and Yamamura, 2003; Charkham, 1995), which means that employees will tend to stay with the same company until their retirement. ESOPs provide part of the incentive for employees to stay with the same company for many years. ESOPs combined with life-long employment also provide the incentives for employees to hold their shares for the long term, making the company's shareholdings relatively stable (Proctor and Miles, 2002).

Although there is only a one-tier board in the Japanese corporate governance system, this does not mean that employees play a less important role than they do in the German co-determination system. The revised Japanese Commercial Code of 1951 required that board members should not be owners of a company but should see themselves as representatives of the interests of the firm; this is akin to the situation of employees (Sakuma, 2001: 143).

The 'stable shareholding' and the interlocking nature of share ownership has effectively rendered the Japanese general shareholders' meeting almost a mere formaility (Charkham, 1995) or a 'rubber stamp' (Proctor and Miles, 2002). Many crucial issues are often resolved in regular meetings (Proctor and Miles, 2002: 111) with the company's stable shareholders (such as suppliers, creditors and customers), who also have a general business relationship with the company. More than one-third of shares are in the hands of financial institutions, such as banks and insurance companies (Sakuma, 2001: 140). Banks therefore play an important role in corporate governance in Japan. Japan's history of relying more on credit finance rather than on equity finance has given banks a crucial role in corporate governance, especially in terms of monitoring company management. Often, companies belonging to the same corporate group (*keiretsu*) have a common 'main bank' as their credit provider. This is illustrated by Proctor and Miles, who noted that:

> [The main bank] may exert control over management in a variety of ways. Its personnel may sit on the company's board of directors. It may hold regular meetings with the management of companies and may ask to be kept informed of plans, policies and activities. In times of crisis, banks may not only inject more capital into the company, they may even take over the management on a temporary basis. . . In the last resort, banks may even decide whether the company continues to trade or is liquidated. They are thus 'crisis managers, allocators of capital and gatekeepers to bankruptcy' all at the same time. (Proctor and Miles, 2002: 115)

However, the monitoring role played by the main bank also has its limitations, most importantly, that it can only provide so-called "state-contingent" governance (Okabe, 2002: 47); this means that the main bank's governance and monitoring role can only be effective when the firm is in financial distress (Okabe, 2002: 47). When the firm is performing well, the bank will not provide much monitoring; this is more or less related to the failed monitoring role of the banks in the bubble period of the late 1980s (Okabe, 2002). Furthermore, the main bank may play a less central role in the twenty-first century (Hoshi and Kashyap, 2001: 7) mainly due to the shrinkage in bank deposits (Hoshi and Kashyap, 2001: 319). Overall, the current exploration of the Japanese model helps us to understand institutional arrangements in Japan and how these could be applied to transitional economies such as China (Aoki, 2000). It is clear that the designers of China's current corporate laws and corporate governance models have learned much from the Japanese experience in these areas (Milhaupt and West, 2004).

MAJOR IMPLICATIONS OF CORPORATE GOVERNANCE MODELS IN CHINA AND AUSTRALIA

Due to the fact that the corporate governance model found in Australia is often believed to be a subset of the outsider-based model, and the Chinese model is seen to be related to the insider-based model, the preceding overview of the major models provides a starting point for the comparative analysis conducted in this chapter. However, each country's system still has its own characteristics; this is clearly the case in regard to Australian corporate governance as well as to corporate governance in China.

Although the corporate governance model found in Australia is often treated as a subset of the Anglo-American model, Australian corporate governance has some unique features of its own (Cheffins, 2002a: 17). By providing case studies of leading resources companies in Australia, we seek to shed some light on the "distinctive political, ideological and legal environment" related to corporate governance in Australia (Cheffins, 2002a: 17).

There has been a debate in China in recent years as to which corporate governance model should be followed by China. Due to the fact that the actual model adopted in China has been influenced by both German and Japanese experiences (the insider-based model), as well as by the US and the UK model (the outsider-based model), China may well fall into a stand-alone category that may typically be termed "corporate governance with Chinese characteristics" (Farrar, 2005: 468). In terms of ownership and control, the dominant corporate governance model found in China could well be described as an insider-based model, with the main characteristic being a dominant shareholder, as found in the majority of China's listed resources companies.

The situation is however in a state of flux; after more than two years since the reform on the split ownership structure was carried out, previously non-tradable shares have gradually been released to the market. This may lead to changes in the ownership structures and corporate governance models in China in the not too distant future.

Nevertheless, at present, the Chinese government is still the major shareholder in most major listed companies, especially in companies that are of strategic importance to the economic development of China; this may be compared to the situation in both Germany and Japan, where the dominant participants in corporate governance are usually banks. China also shares another feature of the German model, namely, that listed companies in China are required by law to set up a supervisory board comprising representatives of employees who are appointed by shareholders (Dahya et al., 2003). However, the functionality of the supervisory board in China has often been questioned; as Dahya et al. have found, the supervisory board can only be effective if it acts as an independent watchdog, something that it is generally not equipped to do in the current Chinese situation.

Another important point about China's current corporate governance model is that China might find it convenient to follow the German model due to some similarities in the economies of both countries. Thus, after 1978, China adopted a so-called "socialist market economy," a concept that is similar to what has been described in the 1991 Annual Report of the Federation of German Stock Exchanges as "the social market economy" (Charkham, 1995: 8) that has been adopted by Germany.

It can be said that China before 1997 had largely followed the Japanese model, but more recently, this approach has changed due to the influence of former Premier Zhu Rongji and his view that the market should now play a major role (Brahm, 2003). Apart from the supervisory board, China's formal corporate governance structures and arrangements now have much in common with those of the Anglo-American model (Tam, 1999: 48). This is evident in the increasing role of stock exchanges and share trading in its market.

As China's economic reforms are occurring in a period of transition, the final corporate governance model that will emerge will depend on how many of the shares owned by the government will actually be released to the wider market. If the Chinese government chooses to eventually sell all its shares to the market, the system will either change to one with a more dispersed-ownership structure (as in the outsider-based model), or into one with a dominant shareholder (non-government) holding the majority of shares, as found in the insider-based model.

In Australia's case, overall, the prevailing corporate governance model of listed companies is generally characterized by a resort to a one-tier board and by a dispersed-ownership structure; these are among the major characteristics of the outsider-based model. Other important reasons for treating this corporate governance model as part of the outsider-based model are that Australia has a "shareholder economy" and that the stock market is a well-established feature of the corporate economy (Cheffins, 2002a: 14). However, due to the number of larger shareholders and institutional investors holding shares in Australian companies, only about half of all Australian listed companies are subject to the same pressures of an outsider system of corporate governance compared with the position in the UK (Stapledon, 1996b: 188). Therefore, Australia does not possess as pure an outsider system as is to be found in the UK or the US (Cheffins, 2002b).

Furthermore, the size of the Australian stock market is relatively small compared with those in the US and the UK. According to statistics from the Australian Stock Exchange in 2003 there were only 1,477 companies listed on this exchange in Australia, with a total market capitalization of around AUS$1.1 trillion (Australian Stock Exchange, 2003). Another Australian feature is that, among its top 500 companies, about 40 either had their head offices or the bulk of their sales outside of Australia (Kiel and Nicholson, 2003).

Understanding the unique characteristics of corporate governance models in China and Australia has paved the way for further analysis of corporate governance in leading resources companies in China and Australia. The following sections will explore corporate governance practices in leading resources companies in China and Australia, with a focus on ownership structures and board composition.

OWNERSHIP STRUCTURE IN LEADING RESOURCES COMPANIES IN CHINA AND AUSTRALIA

Ownership Structure in Leading Resources Companies in China

The ownership structures of listed resources companies in China are dominated by two types of state-owned shares; they are state shares and state-owned legal person shares.[3] State shares and state-owned legal person shares are generally non-tradable in the market and the transfer of these shares has to follow strict rules and this could previously only occur between state-owned enterprises.

However, since the initial release in November 2002 of the 'Circular on Issues Associated with the Sale of State-owned Shares and Legal Person Shares of Listed Companies to Foreign Investors', issued jointly by the China Securities and Regulatory Commission (CSRC), the Ministry of Finance and the State Economic and Trade Commission (SETC, the predecessor of the State-owned Assets Supervision and Administration Commission [SASAC]), foreign investors have been allowed to purchase state shares and state-owned legal person shares under strict rules and procedures (CSRC et al., 2002). In the long run, this may change the ownership structures of listed companies; however, in the interim, this initiative is yet to have much effect on the ownership structure of listed resources companies in China.

Another policy measure that has influenced the ownership structure of listed companies in China is the introduction of a Qualified Foreign Institutional Investor (QFII) scheme into China's domestic stock market. Talks on selling legal person shares to foreign investors started as early as 2001 (People's Daily Online, 2001). Now a QFII scheme will allow foreign investors to purchase A-shares in companies listed on the Shanghai and Shenzhen Stock Exchanges. Overall, QFII shares in a particular company must not exceed 10% of the total shares in the company (China Securities Regulatory Commission and People's Bank of China, 2002: 5). Some QFIIs have already started trading actively in the A-share market, as illustrated by the ownership structure of Baosteel (see Chapter 6). However, in terms of QFIIs' influence on corporate governance, they have yet to have a dramatic influence on the corporate governance of the companies in which they invest.

As we saw in Chapter 1, another policy that could potentially influence current ownership structures in listed resources companies in China arises from the reform initiated in 2005 by the government in seeking to convert non-tradable state-owned shares into tradable shares, and to eventually make these freely tradable in the market.

Major share ownership patterns in the ten leading resources companies in China in both 2004 and 2007 are set out in Tables 3.2 and 3.3.

Table 3.2   Major Share Ownership in Listed Resources Companies in China in 2004

Company name	Major shareholder	Percentage of shares owned	Share type
China Petroleum & Chemical Corporation (Sinopec)	China Petrochemical Corporation	67.92%	State-owned
PetroChina Company Limited	China National Petroleum Corporation (CNPC)	90%	State-owned
Minmetals Development Co., Ltd.	China Minmetals Corporation	71.7%	State-owned
Baoshan Iron & Steel Co., Ltd.	Baosteel Group	85%	State-owned
CNOOC Limited	China National Offshore Oil Corporation (CNOOC)	70.61%	State-owned
Sinopec Shanghai Petrochemical Company Limited	Sinopec Corp.	55.56%	State-owned
Aluminum Corporation of China Limited	Aluminum Corporation of China	42.14%	State-owned
	Non-tradable shares held by other state-owned enterprises	27.99%	
Beijing Shougang Co., Ltd.	Beijing Shougang Group	84.85%	State-owned
Yanzhou Coal Mining Company Limited	Yankuang Group Corporation Limited	54.33%	State-owned
Nanjing Iron and Steel Co., Ltd.	Nanjing Iron and Steel United Co., Ltd.	70.95%	Corporate

Source: share ownership statistics are drawn from each company's annual report for 2003 and/or 2004.

Table 3.3   Major Share Ownership in Listed Resources Companies in China in 2007

Company name	Major shareholder	Percentage of shares owned	Share type
China Petroleum & Chemical Corporation (Sinopec)	China Petrochemical Corporation	70.84%	State-owned
PetroChina Company Limited	China National Petroleum Corporation (CNPC)	86.29%	State-owned
Minmetals Development Co., Ltd.	China Minmetals Corporation	63.4%	State-owned
Baoshan Iron & Steel Co., Ltd.	Baosteel Group	73.97%	State-owned
CNOOC Limited	China National Offshore Oil Corporation (CNOOC)	64.95%	State-owned
Sinopec Shanghai Petrochemical Company Limited	Sinopec. Corp.	55.56%	State-owned
Aluminum Corporation of China Limited	Aluminium Corporation of China	38.56%	State-owned
	Non-tradable shares held by other state-owned enterprises	18.59%	
Beijing Shougang Co., Ltd.	Beijing Shougang Group	63.24%	State-owned
Yanzhou Coal Mining Company Limited	Yankuang Group Corporation Limited	52.86%	State-owned
Nanjing Iron and Steel Co., Ltd.	Nanjing Iron and Steel United Co., Ltd.	52.31%	Corporate

Source: based on 2007 company annual reports and 2008 interim reports.

All the major shareholders listed in Table 3.2 (apart from Sinopec, which is a listed company itself), were wholly state-owned enterprises. They became major shareholders of listed companies as a result of floating some of their assets when they sought to establish those listed companies. This was the result of one of the core strategies aimed at revitalizing the state-owned sector in China during the current transition period of economic and enterprise reform. As shown in Table 3.2, in 2004, all the shares owned by major shareholders were also non-tradable. The major shareholders listed in Table 3.2 were also subject to administration by SASAC, the State Council agency.

In the long run, the split share structure reform will change the ownership patterns and possibly the corporate governance practices of listed resources companies in China. However, because these non-tradable shares will only become freely tradable in the market after the passage of a certain period of time (normally 24–36 months), it will certainly take longer than this period for the changed ownership structures to have any noticeable effect on corporate governance practices. In fact, as Table 3.3 suggests, despite changes in the percentage of the government's controlling shareholding after the split share ownership strucutre reform, the government is still the controlling shareholder of almost all of these companies. Therefore, the effect of the split structure reforms on the current practices of corporate governance in listed resource companies in China is still somewhat limited.

Ownership Structure in Leading Resources Companies in Australia

In contrast to the concentrated patterns of share ownership favored by listed resources companies in China, the ownership structure of listed resources companies in Australia is more dispersed, as illustrated in Table 3.4. This in part reflects the fact that China's major resources companies would be seen as national champions and would thus be nurtured by government; despite the existence of foreign investment rules, the same protective approach has not been evident in government conduct in Australia. However, before the ownership structure of resources companies in Australia is reviewed, the concept of 'substantial shareholding' needs to be defined. Where a shareholder owns 5% or more of a company's shares, it is known as a "substantial shareholder."[4] Substantial shareholders of listed resources companies in Australia in 2004 and 2007 are listed in Tables 3.4 and 3.5.

Table 3.4   Substantial Share Ownership Pattern in Listed Resources Companies in Australia in 2004

Company name	Substantial shareholder	Percentage of shares owned
BHP Billiton	—	—
Rio Tinto Plc	The Capital Group of Companies Inc.	5.99%
Rio Tinto Ltd.	Tinto Holdings Australia Pty	37.5%
Woodside Petroleum	Shell Energy Holdings Australia	34.27%
WMC Resources	UBS Nominees Pty Ltd.	7.79%
	Deutsche Bank AG	6.4%
BlueScope Steel	—	—
OneSteel	Maple-Brown Abbott Limited	7.70%
Newcrest Mining	Merrill Lynch Investment Managers	6.5%
Minara Resources	Glencore International AG	49.44%
Equatorial Mining	Cogent Nominees Pty Ltd	65.9%
	AMP (Bermuda)	29.89%
Alumina	Commonwealth Bank Group	7.21%

Source: 2004 company annual reports and company websites.

Table 3.5   Substantial Share Ownership Patterns in Listed Resources Companies in Australia in 2007

Company Name	Substantial shareholder	Percentage of shares owned
BHP Billiton	—	—
Rio Tinto Plc	Barclays PLC	4.02%
	The Capital Group of Companies Inc.	3.09%
	Legal & General plc	4.36%
	AXA S.A.	4.86%
	Shining Prospect Pte. Ltd.	12%
Rio Tinto Ltd.	—	—
Woodside Petroleum	Shell Energy Holdings Australia	34.27%
WMC Resources	Delisted in 2005, now part of BHP Billiton	
BlueScope Steel	The Capital Group Companies, Inc.	4.8%
	M&G Investment-Funds	5%
	MIR Investment Management Limited	5.16%
OneSteel	MIR Investment Management Limited	7.32%
Newcrest Mining	Capital Group Merrill	14.56%
	Commonwealth Bank	9.62%
	Lynch & Co. Inc.	9.52%
Minara Resources	Glencore International AG	53.23%
	JP Morgan Nominees Australia Limited	7.69%
Equatorial Mining	Delisted in 2006, was acquired by UK-listed Chilean miner Antofagasta Plc	
Alumina	NWQ Investment Management Company LLC and its affiliates	8.7%
	Commonwealth Bank of Australia	8.32%
	Merrill Lynch & Co., Inc.	7.11%
	Schroder Investment Management Group	5.21%
	Maple-Brown Abbott Limited	5.17%
	Wellington Management Company LLP	5.04%

Source: 2007 company annual reports and company websites.

As evident from Table 3.4, BHP Billiton declared that it had no substantial shareholder on its share register (according to data in its 2004 annual report). In Rio Tinto's[5] case, Rio Tinto plc had a substantial shareholder with 5.99%; and in Rio Tinto Ltd., Tinto Holding (a wholly-owned subsidiary of Rio

Tinto plc) owned 37.5% of Rio Tinto Limited's shares. Woodside Petroleum declared (in its 2004 annual report) that Shell Energy Holdings Australia Limited was its substantial shareholder and it held 34.27% of its shares. Prior to being acquired by BHP Billiton, WMC Resources disclosed (in its 2004 annual report) that UBS Nominees Pty Ltd. and Deutsche Bank AG each respectively held 7.79% and 6.4% of its shares. In the case of BlueScope Steel, there was no substantial shareholder which owned more than 5% of its total shares.

In its 2004 annual report, OneSteel disclosed that Maple-Brown Abbott Limited held 7.70% of its shares. In Newcrest Mining, Merrill Lynch Investment Managers held 6.5% of its shares on August 31, 2004. In Minara Resources, Glencore International AG held 49.44% of its shares on March 15, 2005. In Equatorial Mining, Cogent Nominees Pty Limited and AMP (Bermuda) held 65.90% and 29.89% of Equatorial Mining's shares, respectively. However, the beneficiary of Cogent Nominees' shares was Quay Mining Pty Limited, a wholly-owned subsidiary of AMP Life Limited, and AMP (Bermuda) Ltd. is also a wholly-owned subsidiary of AMP Life Limited, which effectively means that 95.79% of its shares were controlled by AMP Life Limited. In Alumina, Commonwealth Bank Group held 7.21% of its shares on February 15, 2005.

It is interesting to see that in 2007, a small number of Australian resources companies actually had substantial shareholders, despite the percentage of shares held being quite small when compared with the size of share ownership by controlling shareholders of Chinese resources companies. While it is outside of the scope of the current discussion to examine whether these institutional investors will play an active role in corporate governance, their record of involvement in corporate governance debates within these companies has been poor.

Overall, the data illustrates that in contrast to the concentrated share ownership structure found in China, the share ownership structure of listed resources companies in Australia is significantly more widely dispersed, despite the changes that occurred more recently.

BOARD COMPOSITION IN CHINA AND AUSTRALIA

Board Composition in China

In China's major resources companies, a majority of board members are either full-time executives or employees drawn from the company's 'mother company' or from its connected companies. A minority of the directors are independent (at least superficially). For companies that have a supervisory board, most of the supervisors are drawn from its mother companies (which are also its dominant shareholders) and/or its connected companies. Director independence in listed resources companies in China is hard to assess, but the data set out in Tables 3.6 and 3.7 provides some assistance in this regard.

Table 3.6 Composition of Boards of Directors and Number of Supervisors in Listed Resources Companies in China in 2004

Company name	Total number of directors	Total number of executive and related directors	Number of independent directors	Total number of supervisors	Number of related supervisors	Number of independent supervisors
Sinopec	14	10	4	12	10	2
PetroChina	13	10	3	6	4	2
Minmetals Development	9	6	3	8	8	0
Baoshan Iron & Steel	11	7	4	9	6	3
CNOOC[6]	8	4	4	NA	NA	NA
Sinopec Shanghai Petrochemical	12	8	4	7	5	2
Aluminum Corporation of China	9	6	3	3	3	0
Beijing Shougang	10	7	3	3	NA	NA
Yanzhou Coal Mining	13	9	4	5	5	0
Nanjing Iron and Steel	9	6	3	5	5	0

Sources: the data is extracted from each company's 2004 annual report.

As set out in Tables 3.6 and 3.7, while some changes occurred in relation to the number of directors and supervisors, the percentage of independent directors and independent supervisors has barely changed. In addition, among the 'related supervisors', as set out in these tables, some are also called employee representatives. However, most of the employee representatives also hold senior management positions either within the mother company or within its connected companies; this brings into doubt their true independence. The connected nature of supervisorship in China renders the supervisory board a much less effective and independent tool than it might otherwise be. In fact, research suggests that a supervisory board in China can only be effective if it acts as an independent watch-dog (Dahya et al., 2003); however, this role is not generally evident in the practices of supervisors in China's listed resources companies.

Table 3.7   Composition of Boards of Directors and Number of Supervisors in Listed Resources Companies in China in 2007

Company name	Total number of directors	Total number of executive and related directors	Number of independent directors	Total number of supervisors	Number of related supervisors	Number of independent supervisors
Sinopec	11	8	3	9	7	2
PetroChina	14	9	5	9	7	2
Minmetals Development	11	8	3	6	6	0
Baoshan Iron & Steel	11	6	5	5	5	0
CNOOC[7]	12	7	5	NA	NA	NA
Sinopec Shanghai Petrochemical	12	8	4	7	5	2
Aluminum Corporation of China	8	5	3	3	3	0
Beijing Shougang	11	7	4	3	3	0
Yanzhou Coal Mining Company	13	9	4	5	5	0
Nanjing Iron and Steel	9	6	3	5	5	0

Sources: based on 2007 company annual reports and 2008 interim reports.

Board Composition in Australia

Public company boards in Australia were once dominated by executive directors. However, in recent years there has been a transformation and now most listed resources company boards are dominated by independent directors as illustrated in Tables 3.8 and 3.9.

Comparing Tables 3.8 and 3.9 with Tables 3.6 and 3.7 suggests that independent directors generally dominate the boards of resources companies in Australia, while connected directors usually dominate boards in resources companies in China. However, the fact that independent directors (at least superficially) exist in China, points to some degree of similarity between corporate governance structures in China and Australia. This suggests that corporate governance in resources companies in China to some extent has characteristics of the outsider-based model. Independent directors usually do not exist in insider-based market models. In the cases of Germany and Japan, the board is usually dominated by insiders. However, the degree of real independence of PRC 'independent directors' is open to doubt (Wang, 2004), but this is changing as companies recruit foreign independent directors to sit on their boards.

Table 3.8   Board Compositions in Listed Resources Companies in Australia in 2004

Company name	Total number of directors	Total number of executive and related directors	Number of independent directors
BHP Billiton	11	2	9
Rio Tinto	14	5	9
Woodside Petroleum	10	4	6
WMC Resources	9	2	7
BlueScope Steel	8	1	7
OneSteel	7	1	6
Newcrest Mining	7	1	6
Minara Resources	6	1	5
Equatorial Mining	7	3	4
Alumina	5	1	4

Source: the data are extracted from each company's 2004 annual reports.

Table 3.9   Board Compositions in Listed Resources Companies in Australia in 2007

Company name	Total number of directors	Total number of executive and related directors	Number of independent directors
BHP Billiton	13	1	12
Rio Tinto	15	4	11
Woodside Petroleum	8	3	5
WMC Resources	Was acquired by BHP Billiton in 2005		
BlueScope Steel	8	1	7
OneSteel	8	1	7
Newcrest Mining	8	2	6
Minara Resources	7	4	3
Equatorial Mining	Delisted in 2006, was acquired by UK-listed Chilean miner Antofagasta Plc		
Alumina	5	1	4

Source: 2007 annual reports and company websites.

BOARD COMMITTEES IN CHINA AND AUSTRALIA

One similarity in the corporate governance practices of resources companies in China to those in Australia is to be found in their shared practice of establishing board committees. As in the case of independent directors, board committees do not usually exist in the insider-based model countries (such as German and Japan). The nature of board committees in resources companies in China is listed in Tables 3.10 and 3.11; the nature of board committees in resources companies in Australia is listed in Tables 3.12 and 3.13.

Table 3.10   Board Committees in Listed Resources Companies in China in 2004

Company name	Audit committee	Investment and development committee	Remuneration committee	Health, safety and environmental protection committee	Nomination committee
Sinopec	√	—	√	—	√
PetroChina	√	√	√	√	—
Minmetals Development	—	—	—	—	—
Baoshan Iron & Steel	√	—	√	—	—
CNOOC	√	—	√	—	√
Sinopec Shanghai Petrochemical	—	—	—	—	—
Aluminum Corporation of China	√	√	√	—	√
Beijing Shougang	—	—	—	—	—
Yanzhou Coal Mining	√	—	—	—	—
Nanjing Iron and Steel Ltd.	—	—	—	—	—

Source: the data is extracted from each company's 2004 annual report.

Note: √, indicates a committee has been established;—, indicates that a committee has not been established.

Tables 3.10, 3.11, 3.12 and 3.13 illustrate that there are some similarities in the use of board committees in listed resources companies in China and Australia. As shown in Table 3.10, six of the ten resources companies in China had board committees as did all of the listed resources companies in Australia examined here. However, the fact that some of these Chinese companies are also listed on the New York Stock Exchange and on the Hong Kong Stock Exchange, as well as on China's domestic exchange, means that the establishment of board committees could not be attributed merely to the influence of China's domestic regulatory environment.[8] Foreign influence has clearly been at work as large Chinese companies have sought overseas stock exchange listing. There has also been an improvement in establishing board committees in a few resources companies as listed in Table 3.11.

Table 3.11 Board Committees in Listed Resources Companies in China in 2007

Company name	Audit committee	Investment and development committee	Remuneration committee	Health, safety and environmental protection committee	Nomination committee	Strategic development committee	Information disclosure committee
Sinopec	✓	—	✓	—	✓		
PetroChina	✓	✓	✓	✓	—		
Minmetal Development	✓	—	✓	—	✓	✓	
Baoshan Iron & Steel	✓	—	✓	—	—	✓	
CNOOC	✓	—	✓	—	✓		
Sinopec Shanghai Petrochemical	✓	—	✓	—	—		
Aluminum Corporation of China	✓	✓	✓	—	✓	✓	✓
Beijing Shougang	✓	—	✓	—	✓	✓	
Yanzhou Coal Mining	✓	—	—	—	—	✓	
Nanjing Iron and Steel	✓	—	✓	—	✓	✓	

Source: based on 2007 company annual reports and 2008 interim reports.

Note: √, indicates a committee has been established;—, indicates that a committee has not been established.

Table 3.12   Board Committees in Listed Resources Companies in Australia in 2004

Company name	Audit committee	Remuneration committee	Health, safety and environment committee	Nomination committee	Committee on social and environmental accountability
BHP Billiton	√	√	√	√	—
Rio Tinto	√	√	—	√	√
Woodside Petroleum	√	√	—	√	—
WMC Resources	√	√	—	√	—
BlueScope Steel	√	√	√	√	—
OneSteel	√	√	√	√	—
Newcrest Mining	√	√	√	√	—
Minara Resources	√	√	—	√	—
Equatorial Mining	√	√	—	—	—
Alumina	√	√	—	√	—

Source: the data is extracted from each company's 2004 annual report.
Note: √, indicates a committee has been established;—, indicates that a committee has not been established.

Table 3.13   Board Committees in Listed Resources Companies in Australia in 2007

Company name	Audit and risk committee (or Compliance committee)	Remuneration committee	Health, safety and environment committee	Nomination committee	Committee on social and environmental accountability (or Sustainability committee)
BHP Billiton	√	√	—	√	√
Rio Tinto	√	√	—	√	√
Woodside Petroleum	√	√	—	√	√
WMC Resources	Now part of BHP Billiton				
BlueScope Steel	√	√	√	√	—
OneSteel	√	√	√	√	—
Newcrest Mining	√	√	√	√	—
Minara Resources	√	√	—	√	—
Equatorial Mining	Now part of UK—listed Chilean miner Antofagasta Plc				
Alumina	√	√	—	√	—

Source: 2007 company annual report and company websites.
Note: √, indicates a committee has been established;—, indicates that a committee has not been established.

RELATED PARTY TRANSACTIONS

There was some disclosure of related party transactions by companies in China and Australia. In most cases, the related parties were the mother company or partly-owned subsidiaries of listed resources companies. Full disclosure of transactions among them helped to ensure that the transactions carried out between them were fair and competitive. Although one of the ultimate aims of the disclosure of related party transactions in both countries was to protect the interests of shareholders, the focus adopted has been totally different in the two countries. In Australia's case, the existence of a fairly widely dispersed–share ownership structure gave rise to the so-called "agency problem"; therefore, full disclose of related party transactions helped to protect shareholder interests from manipulation by management, as management is often in de facto control of the corporation in Australia.

In China's case, the disclosure of related party transactions served a slightly different purpose; this was due to the fact that government was the dominant shareholder in most listed resources companies. Although there was a requirement that listed companies should be independent from their mother company (which was usually a wholly state-owned enterprise, as illustrated in Table 3.2), it was not unusual for the controlling shareholder to sometimes exploit its listed arm so as to ensure that it served the former's interest (China Securities Regulatory Commission, 2002; CSRC and SASAC, 2003). That is also why, in China's case, one of the main governance concerns is the protection of the interests of minority shareholders from being exploited by dominant shareholders, by the management and by directors of listed companies through such related party transactions (Tomasic and Andrews, 2007).

SUMMARY

Based on publicly available information, this chapter has analyzed corporate governance disclosure in leading resources companies in China using Australian mining companies as a basis for comparison. It has helped us build an initial picture of corporate governance practices and mechanisms found in leading resources companies in China. However, in order to gain further insights into their governance practices, primary research (such as reliance on interviews with company secretaries and government officials) needs to be conducted to find out the true status of the implementation of corporate governance principles in these Chinese companies. The following chapter (Chapter 4) provides a deeper analysis of governance practices in leading resources companies based on interviews with government officials and key controllers of these resources companies.

4 Are Owners Really in Control?

INTRODUCTION[1]

Looking through the glossy company annual reports and their sometimes rather formulaic corporate governance reporting statements may lead one to ask how well corporate governance is really understood among controllers of China's resources companies. How well are good corporate governance standards practiced in reality? What are the roles of major stakeholders in corporate governance? The discussion in this chapter is based mainly on interviews with controllers of leading resources companies and government officials from China's two mainland stock exchanges and the corporate regulator, the China Securities Regulatory Commission (CSRC); this will help us build a better picture of corporate governance practices within these resources companies in China.

Despite the fact that the concept of corporate governance is still fairly new in China, the interview data analyzed here suggests that most controllers of listed companies do regard corporate governance as being important. Most of the interviewees from the resources sector also ranked corporate governance as being among the most important issues in their companies. As one company secretary interviewed in Shanghai expressed this sentiment:

> Corporate governance is not just a decoration. It is materially important to improving a company's internal quality. It is a kind of soft code, but more important than ISO quality assurance.

However, at the current stage of development in China, corporate governance problems are very widespread and the CSRC is therefore trying to balance many different conflicts of interest in order to solve these problems. For example, this issue was discussed by one of the interviewees, who noted that:

> The principle of 'same share, same right' has not been implemented. So far, government does not have a stable policy on corporate governance. It favours the majority shareholders when it feels that they

need government support. When there are too many complaints in the market, it will then take measures to protect minority-shareholders' interests.

This quote points to the dilemma that the CSRC is facing in its day-to-day work, which was clearly related to the unique share ownership structure found in China, with the government being the major shareholder in most listed resources companies through its holdings of non-tradable shares. In order to gain a better understanding of corporate governance in China's resources sector in the current circumstances, this chapter is organized around seven major themes: the regulatory environment, the implications that can be drawn from a company's ownership structure and its board and board committees, the functions of supervisors and the supervisory board, the functions of independent directors, related party transactions, stakeholders and the role of the union.

THE REGULATORY ENVIRONMENT FOR RESOURCES COMPANIES IN CHINA AND ITS EFFECT ON CORPORATE GOVERNANCE

China's regulatory environment has its own unique characteristics. As discussed in Chapter 2, administrative measures play a bigger role in improving corporate governance in China than do formal legal measures, such as the Company Law. For example, when The Code of Corporate Governance for Listed Companies in China was first issued by the CSRC in 2002, several official announcements were issued by the government to make it compulsory for listed companies to adopt these governance rules.[2] These official announcements were sent directly to the parent companies of some of the listed companies, as it was frequently the case that the parent company of a listed company was a state-owned enterprise (SOE).

Among the ten leading resources companies studied in this book, six[3] had controlling shareholders that were SOEs and were under the direct supervision of the State-owned Assets Supervision and Administration Commission (SASAC), one[4] was a subsidiary of one of the six companies mentioned in Note 3 and two had controlling shareholders that were SOEs under the direct supervision of the sub-branches of SASAC located in Chinese provinces and cities. The only departure from this pattern was Nanjing Iron and Steel Co. Ltd., whose controlling shareholder was not a wholly state-owned company but a company (Nanjing Iron and Steel United Co., Ltd.) controlled by an entrepreneur (Mr. Guo Guangchang) and an SOE (Nanjing Iron and Steel Group Company). As of August 2005, Mr. Guo had a 60% interest in Nanjing Iron and Steel United Co., Ltd. and Nanjing Iron and Steel Group Company had a 40% shareholding. However, before 2003, about 70% of the shares of Nanjing Iron and Steel Co., Ltd. were owned by Nanjing Iron and Steel Group Company, a state-controlled entity.

The overall status of government as controlling shareholder in almost all ten leading resources companies in China as well as being the regulator of the stock market indicates that the government is both a player and a referee in the stock market in China; this makes it inevitable that the governance of these listed companies will be closely intertwined with the governance of the public sector. In fact, the mechanisms used by the CSRC to promote its Code of Corporate Governance in China illustrate that the government relies on its controlling stake in listed companies to gain information from them and therefore to direct and regulate listed companies during this current stage of development.

The administrative measures have long played an important role in the governance of the private as well as the public sector due to the under-development of law in China (Chen, 1994). The controllers of resources companies interviewed were well aware of this intertwining of public sector governance with the governance of listed companies. This was generally the pattern that was also found in other listed companies in China. As noted by a company secretary in Shenzhen, corporate governance problems in China "[not only] involve the supervision agencies but also intervention from the government"; he further added that the law was not really playing a punitive role and that administrative power played a stronger role:

> The current situation in China is that corporate governance rules and regulations were just transplanted from other countries. It might help to improve the practices of corporate governance in listed companies. However, there is no real punitive role played by the Company Law and the administrative measures have played a bigger role.

This view was also expressed by another interviewee in Shenzhen, who noted that "the administrative measures of the government in most cases can have higher power than the laws." In China's case, the weak form of law and the difficulty of utilizing a proper legal system to punish bad corporate governance has meant that only administrative measures would serve as major deterrents against poor corporate governance. In reality, the lack of a proper legal system to punish bad corporate governance behavior has made fighting poor corporate governance a very difficult agenda to implement.

This suggests that the development of a proper regulatory environment for listed companies in China (especially in the area of corporate governance) is still in its infancy. The current early development of China's regulatory environment can also be demonstrated by the CSRC's swiftness in introducing new rules without any real consultation before the rules become effective; as noted by one observer:

The CSRC tends to have new rules and (in) two days it is effective. In another country, you need to have a consultation period and an education period interactive with investors. And in China it is as if (the rules were) issued one day and (became) effective the next day.

Despite the infancy of the regulatory environment for corporate governance in China, the government is often criticized for utilizing a "legalistic approach" in regulating its listed companies. The "legalistic approach" refers to the fact that the government has issued a large number of regulations and, despite the issuance of numerous laws and regulations, a powerful enforcement system still does not exist. This was confirmed by an interviewee in Hong Kong, who observed: "China is taking a legalistic approach to corporate governance; it issues a lot of regulations but is very weak in enforcement." The reason for this is that the "CSRC lacks political clout to enforce corporate governance rules in China."

This apparent legalistic approach also means that the CSRC has been very rigid in its approach to regulating listed companies and there was often no flexibility to allow for corporate governance issues to be dealt with on a case-by-case basis, as one company secretary in Shenzhen complained. However, some interviewees did think that this legalistic approach suited the current stage of development of corporate governance in China. A smaller number of interviewees, on the other hand, also thought that the CSRC did not issue enough rules, when compared to the SEC in the US and the SFC (the Securities and Futures Commission) in Hong Kong.

The intertwining of the legal enforcement system with the administrative system in China can also have an adverse effect on the implementation of corporate governance rules and practices. In fact, the intertwining of the old system and the new system sometimes also hinders the implementation of new rules. For example, although the rules of the CSRC have clearly stipulated the good faith rule for directors and senior managers of listed companies, it can be extremely hard for the CSRC to initiate disciplinary action against anyone who has a higher government ranking than the regulatory commission, such as a company chairman who has a ministerial rank. As one corporate governance researcher in Hong Kong observed:

The chairman of a company is also someone with a ministerial rank. [That means in China's case, most controllers of listed companies are government officials.] So if you are going after someone bigger than you, you have to be damn right about it. Even if you are right, I'm not sure if it is going to happen as the Chinese are obsessed with their hierarchy.

This pattern is certainly evident in the ten resources companies in China studied for this book. Most of the board chairmen of these companies hold ministerial-level rankings and according to government policy, they should have the same benefits and be treated as government officials with the same ranking. This shows that the governance of listed companies is closely intertwined with public sector governance. It also suggests that it could be hard for anyone to take legal action against those government officials who hold high positions in listed companies. This was confirmed by a few interviewees from the resources sector who confirmed that the CSRC was relatively powerless in enforcing directors' liabilities, but most of them did think that despite this, the existence of rules might have an indirect and psychological effect in improving corporate governance.

As expressed by another interviewee, at the current stage of development of corporate governance in China, it is still better to have more rules than no rules. After all, most interviewees from the resources sector think that the current roles played by the CSRC and the stock exchanges are more focused on educating board members rather than punishing wrongdoers. This is probably why "bad corporate governance in China in most cases will only lead to censure rather than being prosecuted by law," as one corporate governance researcher in Hong Kong put it.

Overall, in terms of the role of the CSRC in regulating China's listed companies, there is still much room for improvement. For example, at present, there are no sanctions for cheating small investors. This makes it possible for dominant shareholders to exploit the interests of small shareholders without being punished through the legal system. We have yet to see how well the 2005 amendments to the PRC Company Law will deal with this problem.[5]

In terms of the roles played by the CSRC and the stock exchanges, most interviewees from the resources sector seemed to believe that the CSRC was the policy maker and was more focused on corporate governance. In contrast, the role of the stock exchange was seen to be more focused on regulating information disclosure by listed companies so as to ensure the quality of the information disclosed. To further improve corporate governance in China, there needs to be more effective coordination between the stock exchanges and the CSRC.

In terms of the corporate governance roles played by China's stock exchanges through their listing rules, some interviewees from the resources sector suggested that (as was the case in their companies), listing rules were effective in terms of the listing agreement signed between the stock exchange and the company, because the board members were also required to sign a document acknowledging their liabilities. The stock exchange rules on disclosure have also become more stringent in recent years; as one interviewee from the resources sector expressed this point:

It prescribes not only the basic rules on disclosure requirements but also the rules for disclosure of extraordinary events, disclosure via the Internet and hardcopy and other information that could potentially influence the share price, such as related party transactions, fabrication of accounts and partial listing.

On the other hand, and as expressed by the same interviewee, the

> CSRC has issued a lot of rules and regulations and these rules are very hard to implement, and sometimes the rules of the CSRC are not realistic. The CSRC really needs to recruit personnel who understand the real situation of how a business is operating and can issue realistic rules for the business world.

Overall, the CSRC's role when compared, for example, with the Australian Securities and Investments Commission (ASIC) is very limited and the CSRC has few legal measures available to help it enforce the rules in cases of violation. The only avenue left to the CSRC is to punish the controllers of listed companies and not to allow listed companies to raise more capital from the market, a remedy that is reactive at best. Therefore, compared with the CSRC, ASIC has more powers in disciplining and disqualifying directors and senior management of listed companies.[6]

Overall, the interview data verifies that the regulatory environment in China is characterized by the intertwining of public sector governance and the governance of listed resources companies and that government administrative power in China really plays a dominant role in regulating listed resources companies. This stands in stark contrast to the situation in Australia and other Western countries where there is a strong legal enforcement system and the government only plays the more limited role of putting a proper governance system in place rather than directly intervening with the governance of individual listed companies.

OWNERSHIP STRUCTURE AND CORPORATE GOVERNANCE

Ownership Structure in Listed Companies in China

As we have seen, in China's stock markets, the level of state ownership of shares in listed companies is very high. In 2002, 36% of listed companies had a single state shareholder with equity ownership of more than 50% (Jiang, 2002).[7] In leading resources companies, as demonstrated in Chapter 3, this figure was even higher, with the major shareholders (usually SOEs) owning more than 80% of shares in three companies, owning 70% in another three companies and more than 55% in the remaining companies (except Nanjing Iron & Steel Co., Ltd.).

Overall, the unique ownership structure of listed resources companies in China gives rise to the issue of protecting both the state interest and the interests of minority shareholders. The existence of less well-defined property rights in China also makes this problem more complicated and gives rise to multi-agency problems.

The agency problem is one of the oldest classical problems prevalent in the Anglo-American corporate governance model. In Australia's case, it has led to a greater concern for the protection of minority-shareholders' interests. However, in China's case, it is more complicated. The multi-agency problem refers to the fact that controllers of listed resources companies are usually appointed by the government and represent the interests of the government; also, there may well be a few levels of delegation within the government hierarchy. Along this line of delegation, the interests of the final agent (the managers of listed companies) are highly unlikely to be congruent with those of the major shareholders (usually, the major shareholder is an SOE which represents the interest of the government).

The existence of minority shareholders adds more complications to this problem, as the misconduct of controllers of listed companies could damage the interests of all shareholders (majority and minority) and the controllers of listed companies, as the agents of the government, could also exploit the interests of minority shareholders for the benefit of majority shareholders. That is why a company secretary interviewed in Shenzhen exclaimed, "A clear property right system is very important for the future development of China and for China to have an effective corporate governance system."

The multi-agency problem could lead to moral hazard problems with senior managers. For example, there have been experiments carried out in some listed companies to allow senior managers of a listed company to become the owners of the company through the use of management buy-outs (MBO). Theoretically, the management buyout itself is not a bad way to pursue economic and enterprise reform in China, as the MBO will eventually result in more congruence of ownership and control in the company. However, finding the most appropriate way of using the MBO procedure will be extremely difficult in China, simply because of the possibility that the owners of listed companies could induce ex-ante moral hazard of senior managers of the company, as those managers could deliberately mismanage the company in the short term in order to reduce the share price of the listed company, which could benefit the management team that intends to buy out the company at a lower price.

In 2004, when these interviews were conducted, the split share ownership structure in China was common in listed companies and the existence of tradable and non-tradable shares also meant that different types of shareholders faced different incentives. The market mechanisms could only have an effect on the shareholdings held by minority shareholders who themselves did not have much power in influencing the share price.

The Chinese government started experimenting with the split share structure reforms in May 2005 and has adopted a gradualist approach in introducing these reforms. In 2008, as this book was being completed, almost all listed companies in China had taken up this share ownership structure reform, but there is no sign that the government will reduce its share holdings in key industries, especially in the resources sector. In fact, with the strategic importance of the resources sector to continued economic growth in China, it is anticipated that the government will remain in control in the resources sector for a relatively long period of time.

In 2004, when our interviews were conducted, some of the interviewees suggested that the existence of then tradable and non-tradable shares meant that major shareholders did not care much about corporate governance, because the fluctuations in share prices were of little relevance to them. This was illustrated by an interviewee in Shenzhen, who noted that if a company was controlled by a major shareholder holding non-tradable shares, and this company was not performing well, then the share price would drop, but only minority shareholders would be hurt as the shares held by the major shareholder were not tradable on the market.

Furthermore, as suggested by another interviewee in Shenzhen, because non-tradable shares and tradable shares have different rights in China, in most cases pursuing the best interests of shareholders only means pursuing the best interest of the dominant shareholder (the majority shareholder). This was probably why good corporate governance was seen to be more important to minority shareholders than it was to majority shareholders, as majority shareholders could more readily protect themselves, but minority shareholders could only rely on good corporate governance to protect them, as suggested by a government official interviewed in Shenzhen.

Even if minority shareholders wanted to participate in corporate governance, their minority shareholdings suggested that they would have little time and ability to work towards improving corporate governance within a company. It would be interesting to find out whether this situation has changed or is likely to change, as nearly three years have passed since the government first started its share ownership structure reforms.

Based on the interview data, we also found that in some cases, the controlling shareholder was also unwilling to practice good corporate governance. As stated by one observer, the paradox of conflict of interests between majority shareholders and minority shareholders was also shown by the fact that the controlling shareholder did not want to be too constrained by corporate governance rules. On the other hand, minority shareholders were not able or prepared to invest resources to seek to improve the quality of corporate governance.

The result of this imbalance of power between the majority shareholder and minority shareholders is that the only feasible option left to minority shareholders was for them to 'vote with their feet', if they were dissatisfied with company policy. This is probably why the popular mindset in China is that the stock market is not a place for long-term investment but rather a place for short-term speculative gains. This is probably also why Wu Jinglian, a famous Chinese economist, has suggested that the risk of investing in China's stock market was even higher than playing in a casino. This coincided with a comment expressed by an interviewee in Hong Kong:

> Major shareholders still see practicing good corporate governance as something they are forced to do. Small shareholders really have no control of corporate governance; therefore, they are very speculative, looking for short-term profit gain rather than holding their shares for the long term.

In terms of the situation found in leading resources companies in China, it was also believed (by many of those interviewed) that the distorted ownership structure found in China has led to the fact that probably only holders of tradable shares were really concerned with corporate governance and also with issues such as "whether the company is managed in an efficient way." An interviewee from a resources company said that he felt that holders of non-tradable shares only cared about making money; therefore, the major task in improving corporate governance in China is to first improve the share ownership structure.

From his own experience, one interviewee from the resources sector suggested that the current share ownership structure in his own company, as well as in other companies, hindered the improvement of corporate governance. This was because there was currently more of a focus on compliance rather than on voluntary disclosure; he added:

> The majority shareholder is more interested in maintaining control of the listed company. Due to information asymmetry, the investment activities of the public shareholders are similar to gambling. [Therefore], they would like to see improvement in corporate governance.

Because of the imbalance in the share structure, with the existence of a large amount of non-tradable shares, not many avenues are left for the holders of tradable shares or for minority shareholders to tackle corporate governance. As a company secretary of a resources company observed:

> Small shareholders still attach lots of importance to corporate governance, which allows them to put more confidence in the company. But small shareholders do not actively pursue this end and they make a judgment for themselves by selling and buying stocks.

In terms of protecting the interests of minority shareholders, one interviewee from the resources sector put this point directly: "small investors do not have any protection at all, and it is a long way to improving that." Most interviewees also suggested that good corporate governance should help to protect the interests of minority shareholders. A few interviewees also suggested that to really protect the interests of small shareholders, there was a need for easier methods of voting (such as voting via the Internet). In some cases, when it is possible for the dominant shareholder to exploit the interests of minority shareholders, only minority shareholders should be allowed to vote. In companies in the resources sector, a few interviewees confirmed that their companies had arrangements to allow minority shareholders to be the only voters on certain issues (such as on related party transactions and the further allocation of shares).

Despite the fact that it was a common belief that minority- or small-shareholders' interests need protection, a few interviewees from the resources sector took a different view. Many thought that small-shareholders' interests were overemphasized and that it might not be good for the efficient operation of the company. But paradoxically, most of these interviewees also claimed that they did have problems with protecting the interests of minority shareholders, as one company secretary interviewed suggested: "companies have not done enough to protect minority shareholders." This apparent paradox rests on the fact that, on the one hand, they felt frustrated by the legalistic approach taken by the government in prescribing numerous rules and regulations for listed companies to protect minority-shareholders' interests; on the other hand, they saw an apparent gap in practices in protecting minority-shareholders' interests and struggled to find effective ways of dealing with this.

China's unique dominant state share ownership structure has also rendered the shareholders' annual general meeting powerless. This is exemplified in listed resources companies, as was pointed out by one interviewee, who noted that:

> Because the structure of the shares, small shareholders do not have much power to argue and the Annual General Meeting also does not matter, because one vote can decide everything.

One of the interviewees from the resources sector also suggested that the Annual General Meeting in his company only decided on the details of the annual report. Another interviewee from a company in the resources sector, suggested that in his company:

> It is a normal practice to check with the biggest shareholder before an Annual General Meeting. Before a formal meeting, you have lots of informal meetings, so you do not get embarrassed at the formal meeting. This should include communicating with the majority shareholder. . . to ensure that the formal board meeting will operate smoothly and that they sign at the end of the meeting.

Another interviewee from a resources company indicated that the procedure in his company was that the annual general meeting of shareholders was only part of the reporting system: "after the issues have been approved by the annual general meeting, they still have to go through the government to get final approval." This illustrates that government control was still quite important in those listed companies that had been transferred from SOEs. Nevertheless, there are still some situations in the resources sector where companies do not check with the majority shareholder before making a decision (as some interviewees noted).

As the controlling shareholder of most large listed companies, government could be criticized for its role; for example, it could use its position to gain insider information of the company's affairs; also, companies with the best performing assets will be allowed by government to go abroad to raise more capital. This method will ensure that in the initial transition period of China's economic and enterprise reform, most companies selected for overseas listing will have a better chance of success. This will arguably also help to build a better reputation for PRC-controlled listed companies in the international capital market. Those companies with controlling state shareholders that are listed abroad are also acting as a platform and window for controllers and regulators of listed companies in China to help them to learn best practices from aboard.

The Role of Strategic Investors and Institutional Investors

In the case of listed resources companies in China, it was not uncommon for them to have shareholders categorized as "strategic investors."[8] Some of these strategic investors were overseas companies and some were domestic investors. For a particular company, the major role of a strategic investor was to attend the general shareholder meeting and provide advice at the meeting, as one company lawyer interviewed in Beijing confirmed. From the perspective of overseas strategic investors, it was argued that this type of arrangement could also be called an "equity-for-market" deal (Nolan, 2001), as becoming a strategic shareholder of a major resources company would give investors the opportunity to access the retail network of the company, which proved really useful in accessing the fast-growing Chinese market with its stringent rules for foreign investors.

For example, Chalco, the Aluminum Corporation of China Limited, has Alcoa as a strategic investor. As stated in Chalco's 2004 annual report, Alcoa owned 8% of Chalco's H shares. As a strategic investor, Alcoa was allowed to appoint a non-executive director; this practice gave Alcoa the opportunity to access Chalco's crucial sales and marketing information as well as the opportunity to network with other executive directors to facilitate further co-operation in the product market.

In the case of listed resources companies in China, there has also been an interest in encouraging Qualified Foreign Institutional Investors (QFIIs) to invest in those companies. Most interviewees from the resources sector believed that if a QFII was investing in a particular company, this would help to attract domestic investors to the same company, as most domestic investors believed that QFIIs should have done proper research before they invested in that company. This was also why some of the interviewees felt that QFIIs could help to change the speculative investment culture that existed in China. From his own experiences, one interviewee admitted that strategic investors and institutional investors would have more interest in his company's corporate governance than small investors who at most times were only interested in the company's share price.

Despite the positive view of some of the interviewees concerning the role of institutional investors in corporate governance, there did exist another view in the resources sector. One interviewee from the resources sector suggested that institutional investors were not really interested in corporate governance and that they were only interested in making money. As stated by another interviewee from the resources sector, in his own experience with foreign investors who were interested in investing in his company, the foreign investors did not really understand China. The same interviewee also suggested that foreign investors could have more impact on the listed company's investment skills and knowledge, rather than on its corporate governance practices. This also coincided with the views of other interviewees who thought that the main aim of the QFII scheme was to make money rather than to improve corporate governance practices.

THE FUNCTIONS OF THE BOARD AND
THE BOARD COMMITTEES

In order to gain a better understanding of the composition and the functions of the board and its committees in resources companies, we have reviewed biographical data on the board members and the senior management team of each company (as disclosed in company annual reports and their respective websites).

These biographies reveal that most executive and non-executive directors received fairly good educations in China but that not many of them had studied overseas. Among all of these companies, CNOOC was an exception as many of its directors and senior personnel received a foreign education; this included the chairman of the company who studied at the University of California. The chief financial officer (CFO) of CNOOC received all of his education overseas and worked for various renowned international investment banks before joining CNOOC.

In terms of board composition, in most cases, the chairman of the listed company was also the chairman and CEO of the 'mother company' (usually this company was an SOE), indicating that the listed company was still under the tight control of the government. In most of these companies, a majority of the executive directors and non-executive directors were also senior managers in the mother company and the remainder were senior managers of the listed company; this again suggested that the management of a listed company was very much intertwined with the management of its mother company.

For example, in Baoshan Iron & Steel Co., the chairman of the board was also the chairman and the CEO of the mother company, Baosteel Group Company (an SOE), and interestingly, the website of Baoshan Iron & Steel showed that the chairman of Baoshan Iron & Steel Co. was described as Executive Director (although she has no official position in the listed company). Similarly, the chairman of China Minmetals Development was the CEO and Party Secretary of the mother company, China Minmetals Corporation (an SOE). In fact, for much of their career, most of the executive and non-executive directors and senior management team of these resources companies have worked for the mother company of the listed company before the new company was listed.

The above analysis has huge implications for the roles played by the chairman and the directors of the board and for the functioning of a listed company as an independent entity. For example, as illustrated on its website, Minmetals Development was often treated as a department of the mother company, rather than as an independent economic entity. This phenomenon coincided with the comments made by most interviewees from the resources sector, who expressed the view that the chairman was the one who "sets the tone" for the company and made major decisions. Interviewees from the resources sector also claimed that executive directors usually had less understanding about corporate governance; as one resources sector interviewee observed: "executive directors are appointed by the government and are not so clear about their responsibilities. . ."

In terms of the appointment of board members, as exemplified by the resources sector, some interviewees confirmed that the board was mainly nominated by the controlling shareholders and that the board had a close connection with the government. This explained why directors had difficulties in protecting the interests of 'the company as a whole'. One resources sector interviewee pointed out that:

> At the start, directors thought in this narrow way (the company's interest as a whole). But over time, this has changed. They bear in mind the interests of the country and the Party. As senior managers, directors always think about the return on equity/capital. This practice is not much different from being a state-owned enterprise.

This illustrates the coexistence of the old management system that was dominated by the party and the new system that is dominated by the board. In fact, most secretaries of the Communist Party in the parent or mother company were also appointed either as the chairman or as a director of the listed company. Overall, the coexistence of the old communist system has two types of effect: on the one hand, the new system functions awkwardly in coexistence with the old system; on the other hand, with the gradual establishment of the new system, the existence of the old system has provided a communication channel and gives the power to force through new concepts and practices of corporate governance, although the new system is being established very slowly.

In terms of the establishment and the functioning of board committees, the audit committee was the most frequently established committee in China's listed companies. In China's resources companies, six of the ten companies examined here have established audit committees. In terms of the composition of audit committee, they were normally led by an independent director and were mainly composed of independent directors. Most interviewees also stated that it is important for the audit committee to monitor the company's auditors because if auditors want to cheat investors it is easy to do so and the punishment for doings this is relatively small.

Audit committees really played important roles in corporate governance in some resources companies. For example, in one resources company, the company secretary noted that the audit committee performed four major functions:

[The audit committee in my company] establishes an internal control system, recruits external auditors, reviews financial reports before they are sent to the board, and the audit committee also audits performance of the management team.

In some of the listed companies, the audit committee was effective in protecting minority-shareholders' interests, but, as suggested by one interviewee, this also depended on who was the chair of the audit committee. Another interviewee from a resources sector company suggested that the audit committee in his company had not as yet produced many positive outcomes.

THE FUNCTIONS OF SUPERVISORS AND THE SUPERVISORY BOARD

Unlike the supervisory board in Germany, the supervisory board as it operates in China is mainly composed of internal supervisors, employee representatives and, in the case of big SOEs, the supervisory board will also include outside supervisors from the government (Li, 2007: 9).

In the case of leading resources companies, most of them have established a supervisory board, as required by the Company Law; the only exception is CNOOC.[9] To help better understand the role played by supervisors and the supervisory board in resources companies, the biographies of the supervisors of leading resources companies were also reviewed. Overall, members of the supervisory board normally worked as the union leader or as the secretary of the Communist Party in the mother company, and few were involved in the company's operations or in the actual day-to-day business management of the company.

Usually, the chairman of the union was also appointed as the chairman of the company's supervisory board; but because the union is established and controlled by the party and the government, the chairman of the union is not independent and therefore does not solely represent the workers' interests. This also suggests that it is highly unlikely that the union leader (usually the chairman of the supervisory board) will stand up and act against the major shareholder of the company. As one interviewee observed:

[In mainland China], the unions are very close to the party, i.e., to the government; therefore, they may have a different agenda from protecting the interests of employees. The only way to prove that the union is really functioning is that employees are allowed to be on strike, which rarely happens in mainland China.

This point was also made by another interviewee from the resources sector:

The union may protect employee interests but only to a certain extent. In China, you hardly ever hear that workers are on strike as unions are led by the government.

A company lawyer from a resources company also expressed the view that "the union plays an important role only when the company deteriorates. When the company is growing, they play little role." Most interviewees from resources companies suggested that unions in China had no decisionmaking power at all. One interviewee also suggested that the union's role was mainly for employee welfare and that its role was really "nominal and minor."

However, there was something interesting happening in this space. As from May 2005, workers from an iron and steel company (Panzhihua Iron and Steel Group) were allowed to elect their own union leaders (People's Daily Online, 2005d). Whether the newly elected union members will be willing to confront the majority shareholder—the government and the management team appointed by the majority shareholder—is another matter. Nevertheless, this innovation may lead toward a more functional union which could better represent the interests of employees.

In China's resources companies employee representatives are appointed to the supervisory board by the majority shareholder, and most of them also hold various senior positions either with a subsidiary of the listed company or with an affiliate of the listed company. The close connection of supervisors to the mother company and its affiliates helps to explain why many people do not think that the supervisory board is effective. This view was expressed by one interviewee as follows:

The supervisory board is there just to be there. Employee representatives are accountable to the chairman and they don't give any independent advice, and they are there just to sign off. We never see any effective action from the supervisory board. On the other hand, independent directors are normally professionals; therefore, they have a better understanding about their responsibilities.

These comments are generally in line with other research on the functions of the supervisory board in China. For example, Dahya et al. (2003) found that the supervisory board could only be effective when it was acting as an independent watchdog.

As noted in Chapter 3, the existence of a supervisory board is one of the major characteristics of the insider-based model, as is evident from the development of this model in listed companies in Germany. In contrast, the existence of independent directors is one of the major features of the Anglo-American model. However, in China's listed companies, not only does a supervisory board exist, but independent directors are also required to be appointed to the board; normally, independent directors will comprise a third of all directors.

Whether the supervisory board and independent directors will function effectively is outside the scope of the present analysis, but as an interviewee pointed out, the overlapping functions of the supervisory board and independent directors have made the responsibility of the supervisory board and independent directors unclear and confusing. Sometimes company secretaries are often frustrated by the complicated system of independent directors that coexists with a supervisory board. This sentiment was expressed by a company secretary interviewed in Beijing:

The main task of directors is to make decisions. Supervisors are not there to make decisions. Therefore, they are not under pressure like the independent directors. In China, the supervisory board has nothing to do. In practice, we do not know how to make full use of that board. If we want to pass a resolution, to whom should we pass the matter first for discussion, the board of directors or the supervisory board? I think the supervisory board should discuss matters first and make a decision. But how can we put their opinions to the meeting of the board of directors? There is no mechanism for this. We haven't yet designed a good system as the supervisory board only reports to the shareholder general meeting. It has no power to pass opinions to the board of directors. . .

These remarks coincide with a comment made by another company secretary of a resources company interviewed in Shanghai:

Within our structure, we can't find a good place for the supervisory board. In our company, we have this problem of how to relate the supervisory board to the shareholders' general meeting and the board.

Most interviewees also expressed the view that independent directors played a far more important role in their companies than the supervisory board. As a company secretary in Shenzhen said: "the supervisory board is unnecessary." Most interviewees really think that the supervisory board actually dilutes the function of the board. In another resources company, the interviewee suggested that the supervisory board did not play a substantial role in corporate governance because all supervisory board members were drawn from the parent company.

Despite the less functional role in corporate governance played by the supervisory board, an interviewee from a resources company revealed that the function of the supervisory board in his company had been strengthened dramatically after it was reviewed by an internationally renowned consulting organization and suggestions were made to change the function of the supervisory board. These were accepted, as explained by this interviewee:

> At present (and after the review), areas examined by our supervisory board include the implementation of the Annual General Meeting's resolutions, company financial system, human resource management and related party transactions.

Overall, most interviewees suggested that the major role of the supervisory board in their respective companies was to supervise the accounting department and to monitor if the general manager is acting in compliance with the law, and also to review special events. Supervisors are more likely to play a monitoring role than to directly participate in the decisionmaking process of a listed company, in contrast to supervisory boards in Germany.

Overall, the preceding discussion suggests that in China's case, although there are signs that the supervisory board's role in corporate governance is improving, because the members of the supervisory board are appointed by the majority shareholder, it will be some time before the supervisory board is really functional in corporate governance terms.

THE FUNCTIONS OF INDEPENDENT DIRECTORS

As suggested recently by the chairman of China Life, boards of directors should include experts in related fields that would benefit the company and would be mainly composed of independent directors (Chao, 2007). According to the biographies of independent directors of China's resources companies (as disclosed in annual reports and their respective websites), most independent directors were professionals; they were either legal professionals, experts in the company's industry or in accounting and/or auditing. It was suggested by most resources sector interviewees that one of the important roles of independent directors in listed companies in China was to provide professional advice, such as accounting, auditing and legal advice, to the listed company. This was consistent with the fact that most controllers of listed companies were transferred from previous positions held in SOEs before their companies were listed on the stock exchange. Therefore, their experiences tended to be more firm specific; on the other hand, independent directors were generally professionals and complemented the skills of the controllers of listed companies. Interviewees from a number of resources sector companies also suggested that independent directors had professional skills that could not only benefit the company but could also help other directors nominated by the majority shareholder to understand corporate governance.

Despite the fact that some of the interviewees concluded that independent directors played a better role in corporate governance than the supervisory board, in most cases, independent directors were criticized for not functioning properly. The fact that independent directors often have a very close relationship with the dominant shareholder has undermined their potential to oversee proper management of related party transactions and the appointment of senior officers. This was confirmed by interviewees from the resources sector. This also coincided with a comment from one interviewee that independent directors might not be truly independent as they were chosen by the dominant group on the board and rewarded by that group. In China, independent directors were often branded as "beautiful vases," as it was said that they were only appointed for decorative purposes in the boardroom. Paradoxically, even if independent directors want to contribute more to corporate governance, their independent status somehow undermines their ability to monitor corporate governance of the company; this is because they have limited information about the company compared with the vast amount of information readily available to the executive directors. As one of the interviewees pointed out:

> [The] independent director can only get information from the board of directors' meeting, and the information they get is only what the management directors choose to give them and only on paper; therefore, they do not really have the strength [knowledge] to speak at the board of directors' meeting, so most of them choose to be silent.

This limited access to important information is also known as the "asymmetry of information problem," as independent directors will have much less information than the executive directors, who work on a day-to-day basis in the company. This also makes it hard for independent directors to monitor corporate governance–related issues, such as the real financial status of the company, and whether there have been any unlawful related party transactions.

The role played by independent directors also varies slightly across companies. In the case of the resources sector, some interviewees indicated that independent directors played an important role in board meetings and that they offered their opinions and were willing to ask questions rather than just come and read whatever information they have been given. As suggested by John Thornton, the former president of Goldman Sachs and an independent director of China Netcom and Industrial and Commercial Bank of China, (independent) directors should also work within the context of China and make their contribution by providing significant input to the board's decision-making process, which is normally dominated by executive directors and party representatives (Barton and Huang, 2007).

In terms of protecting minority-shareholders' interests, in one resources company, the comment was made that independent directors could effectively represent minority shareholders, and that there have been cases where independent directors did stand up and speak out:

> There have been some cases in which independent directors opposed the executive directors, e.g., by refusing to sign off on a proposal. This has sent a message to the market that independent directors can speak out against the board. When such a situation arises, sometimes the independent director will be dismissed by the board.

Although the end result might not be that positive (as the independent director was eventually dismissed), it at least suggests that there are signs that the function of the independent director is improving. Another illustration of this point was given by an interviewee who noted that independent directors often resigned over not being given enough information. It was suggested that this indicated that independent directors did play a role in corporate governance and that if this was so, it was a role with limited effectiveness. However, there is a paucity of suitable independent directors in China so that their resignation leads to other problems in finding suitable replacements.

RELATED PARTY TRANSACTIONS AND CORPORATE GOVERNANCE

Related party transactions in China's listed companies have been a matter of major concern because of unclear property rights and multi-agency problems. As suggested by one interviewee, representatives (the agents) of state shareholders in a listed company sometimes engage in related party transactions for their own benefit, and it is also not uncommon for a listed company to use related party transactions to falsely increase profits, or to transfer profits from a listed company to its holding company or to subsidiaries of the holding company. This arises because listed companies are sometimes not really independent of their holding companies, as was often noted by interviewees. Also, there exist many legitimate transactions between listed companies and their subsidiaries or with subsidiaries of their holding companies. This means that it is even harder to detect whether related party transactions are fair and at arm's length.

The existence of legitimate related party transactions between a listed company and its related parties can often be justified or explained historically. A listed company and its related parties normally belonged to a whole group of closely related SOEs before any SOE within the group was listed. Therefore, numerous social and business ties between them continued to exist after a company in a group of SOEs is listed. This explains the perceived legitimacy of some related party transactions. In other cases, to ensure the success of a listed company, its parent company sometimes also supports its revenue growth through related party transactions, as one interviewee suggested. This illustrates that most listed companies still receive strong support from government (as most parent companies remain SOEs). This practice ensures the success of listed companies in the stock market— thereby, minimizing the risks that are inherent in the wider economic and enterprise reform process in China. It shows that listed companies that have been transformed from SOEs are still utilized as vehicles to implement government policies in China; interestingly, this type of practice may sometimes benefit minority shareholders, as one interviewee observed. However, not all related party transactions are beneficial to minority shareholders.

Related party transactions can also arise where a listed company provides loans to its parent company. This occurs because when a listed company seeks listing, it is usually allocated the best performing assets from its parent company so that it can be successfully listed in the stock market. This practice, leaves the unlisted parent company with less well-performing assets, therefore, making it harder for the unlisted parent to further secure its bank loans. Not surprisingly, a listed subsidiary is seen as the last resort by its parent company when seeking financial support and it will be hard for a listed company to refuse such a request. Furthermore, statistics have shown that in 2005, over 90% of listed companies provided loans to their unlisted parents (Su, 2005).

The resources sector is no exception to this pattern of conduct. As expressed by an interviewee from a resources company, because a listed company was packaged with the best assets from its parent company and its subsidiaries, the parent company and its subsidiaries were often left with non-performing assets, so that sometimes the related party transaction was also used to channel profits from the listed companies into the parent company or to other entities that were under the control of the parent company (Hu, 2007). This has emerged as one of the major regulatory dilemmas in dealing with related party transactions.

Many controllers of listed companies believe that it is important to draw a clear line between related party transactions that are normal business transactions and related party transactions that undermine the rights of minority shareholders. Most controllers of listed companies believe that the assets of a government-controlled listed company belong to the mother company (usually it is unlisted) and in the end, to the government; sometimes, controllers of listed companies also feel that there is nothing wrong with inter-company loans within the same corporate group. As one interviewee observed:

> They'd think, "I am just moving money around for the whole company and what's wrong with that?" Of course, they are different companies and when they are doing that without consulting minority shareholders, only small-shareholders' interests will suffer.

Another problem with related party transactions is that the company is forced to make such transactions as a result of pressure from the major shareholder; as an interviewee from the resources sector noted:

> There is big pressure from the majority shareholder, as the chairman is nominated by the majority shareholder. It is easier for a listed company to deal with its subsidiary company than its parent company.

Related party transactions in listed resources companies can also be used as a means to access major resources provided by their parent companies, as noted by one interviewee. The listed company can however become too dependent on its parent company, as one interviewee from a resources sector company acknowledged:

> The degree of independence of a listed company from its parent company determines the approach adopted by the listed company to corporate governance. Most former SOEs are still dependent on their parent companies. This has led to rampant related party transactions and a lack of real separation of the parent company from the subsidiary.

It was emphasized by one interviewee from the resources sector that his company had related party transactions with other companies in the same corporate group, but he said that there were no related party transactions with company directors. However, another interviewee in the resources sector revealed that there did exist cases in which related party transactions were manipulated through the setting up of another company or the use of another name by directors, and "companies may also use inside information for related party transactions," as suggested by another interviewee.

Overall, related party transactions constitute a very difficult corporate governance problem, as acknowledged by one interviewee from the resources sector:

> It is very hard to say if (the) board can appropriately deal with related party transactions because of China's specific situation. Currently,

most listed companies are state-owned and the controlling shareholders act as representatives of the state. The majority of companies are conducting related party transactions. The related party transaction is probably the main problem facing all large listed companies. They cannot deal with this systemic problem by themselves.

In the resources sector, there is also another view. Because many companies are also listed on the New York, London or Hong Kong Stock Exchanges, more stringent rules on related party transaction applied to companies listed there. One interviewee from a resources company in China observed that the CSRC has started to impose higher standards for related party transactions; for example, independent directors could state their own opinions of a transaction and publish these in newspapers.

Overall, related party transactions in China are complicated and carry the burden of the history of the development of listed companies from their origins as SOEs. Managing and regulating related party transactions properly in China is also a key to the success of economic and enterprise reform, as well as a key to the further development of good corporate governance in China.

THE ROLE OF STAKEHOLDERS IN CORPORATE GOVERNANCE IN LISTED RESOURCES COMPANIES

Apart from shareholders, the board and the management, other stakeholders are also important in promoting good corporate governance. It is therefore appropriate to look at this wider stakeholder role in corporate governance. Interestingly, in companies in the resources sector, when interviewees were asked to identify their most important stakeholders, most thought that shareholders were the most important stakeholders. Some interviewees also pointed out that the most important stakeholders were the parent corporation, government, management, employees and the municipal government (and in this order of importance). They also noted that employees were only relatively minor stakeholders of the company and that the protection of employee interests was not seen as an urgent concern. A board secretary of a resources sector company interviewed in Beijing suggested that the most important stakeholders were, first, shareholders, then the public interest and, finally, employees. Most interviewees stated that the shareholder's interests came first, referring in this regard to the dominant shareholder.

Some other interviewees from the resources sector also believed that shareholders and customers were most important stakeholders, and sometimes they pointed to the parent company and ultimately to the government. A few interviewees from the resources sector identified the government as their most important stakeholder because not only was the government the major shareholder in most companies, it also played another important role in the resources sector—that of allocating natural resources among different companies. This illustrates that under China's unique "socialist market economy," government intervention still plays a major function as a substitute for free market competition. One interviewee in a resources company held a slightly different view; he believed that the most important stakeholders were customers, then the media, the banks and potential investors. Some interviewees from the resources sector also thought that the important stakeholders were not only the dominant shareholders and strategic investors, but also employees who had a stronger sense of ownership in companies that had been transformed from SOEs.

In terms of stakeholder involvement in corporate governance, this should be looked at from two perspectives: first, whether stakeholders are actively involved in corporate governance; and second, where stakeholders are not so actively involved, whether their interests have been protected. Although, some leading resources companies had supervisors who were described as employee representatives, because employee representatives usually held senior positions either with the listed company, its mother company or with their affiliates, it was doubtful whether they could play a major role in representing the interests of general employees. In terms of whether employees also actively participated in corporate governance, one interviewee from a resources company admitted that ordinary workers were not so important in participating in corporate governance:

> Corporate governance is there to establish a system that keeps decision making efficient and correct. That leads the company to survive and develop. Workers are far away from this, but we need the help of workers and must take them into account. Now we pay more attention to scientists and investors, not just workers.

This comment illustrates that although employee interests will probably be considered when seeking to achieve good corporate governance, the actual involvement of employees in corporate governance is really very limited. Therefore, although a company in China has a supervisory board that is modelled on the system of corporate governance found in Germany, the actual involvement of employees in the governance of the company is far smaller than that found in Germany. Also, as an interviewee from the resources sector observed, because the employee representatives on the board in his company were also senior managers of the subsidiaries (based on information disclosed in 2004 annual reports and information disclosed on company websites), it was hard for those employee representatives to really represent the interests of ordinary workers.

In terms of protecting the interests of employees, an interviewee noted that his company had established a proper incentive system and had tried to improve employee living standards as well as to improve their working conditions. Some of the interviewees also admitted that the practices of protecting the best interests of employees in their companies were related to the fact that their companies were once large SOEs before their listing, and historically, protecting employee interests and providing for the social welfare of employees was seen as part of their company culture. It was admitted by another interviewee from a resources company that special arrangements to protect employee interests in his company were indeed very closely related to the fact that his company had been transformed from an SOE, and special care was taken to balance the interests of employees during the transition period:

> Special care should be provided to those (employees) who have worked 20 to 30 years for the former state-owned enterprise under very low wages. They are no longer competitive. . .but have very precious experiences. So we treat them differently from new employees working under new contracts.

Despite the special care that might be provided to employees, some interviewees from the resources sector stressed that employee protection needed to be balanced with shareholder interests and that shareholder interests had to be given priority. Another interviewee from the resources sector stated that listed companies that had been transformed from SOEs are still treated as vehicles for the government to maintain social stability, and to provide support to the social welfare system as the company's care for their employees imposes less of a burden on the government.

This approach was in line with the fact that although most interviewees did not see employees as their most important stakeholders, employees in listed companies that had been transformed from SOEs were seen as a group that were usually well protected as stakeholders in China. Employees in listed companies that had been transformed from SOEs seem to enjoy more de facto rights and protection (Jia, 2004). An interviewee also saw this as the "residual social obligation" of listed companies in China.

Overall, in the resources sector, interviewees saw the major shareholder—the government—as the most important stakeholder. Despite the fact that most interviewees did not think that employees were among their most important stakeholders, largely for historical reasons, employees in the resources sector were often well-protected stakeholders. However, the direct involvement of employees in corporate governance was rather limited as employee representatives on the supervisory board were appointed by the government rather than being elected by a company's employees.

SUMMARY

This chapter has reviewed empirical evidence at firm level in China with an emphasis on the situation in the resources sector.

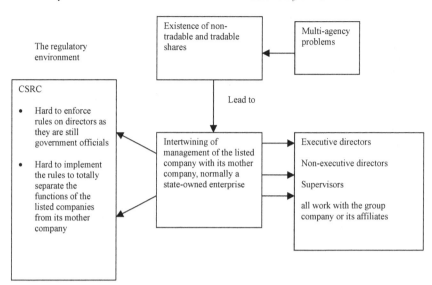

Figure 4.1   Illustration of the intertwining of corporate governance with public-sector management in the resources sector in China.

As demonstrated in Figure 4.1, overall, corporate governance in leading Chinese resources companies is still more or less represented by the reality of strong government control, not only in terms of holding majority shares (most of which are non-tradable), but also by active involvement in managing listed companies through direct appointment of executive directors, senior management teams and members of the supervisory board, as well as by appointment of independent directors. Overall, our conclusions from this data are summarized in Figure 4.1.

The government's active involvement in corporate governance is also represented by the fact that employee representatives on a company's supervisory board are directly or indirectly appointed by the government, and employees' interests are protected mainly following the protocols of the old planned economy. Despite the drawbacks of these practices in China, overall, the current role played by the government in corporate governance is a very important one as it helps to maintain the stability of society during this transition period of the economy and during this period of enterprise reform in China.

5 Corporate Governance in the World's Leading Resources Companies

The Cases of BHP Billiton, Rio Tinto, Shell and Chevron

How do corporate governance practices in China's resources-sector companies compare with industry leaders in other countries? How well advanced are Chinese companies in the process of catching up with best-practice companies across the world? To answer these questions, detailed case studies of BHP Billiton and Rio Tinto, and brief case studies on Shell and Chevron provide a basis of comparison to allow us to evaluate current practices in the leading Chinese resources companies.

OVERVIEW OF THE RESOURCES SECTOR IN AUSTRALIA

The resources industry in Australia has grown rapidly in recent years. In 2002, only three resources companies in Australia's top 500 companies list were ranked among the top 100; in 2004, ten resources companies were included in the top 100 list, with Equatorial Mining moving from number 482 in 2003 to number 41 in 2004 and Minara Resources' ranking moving from number 484 to number 70. In 2008, among the Australian Stock Exchange's (ASX) top 300 listed companies, about 50 were resources companies. The growth of the resources sector in Australia in recent years has contributed to a fast growing Chinese economy, which has in turn generated huge demand pressures on the world resources sector. The corporate governance mechanisms of major listed companies affect the way in which they are seen by securities markets; listed companies are also required to facilitate this by making appropriate disclosures of their governance arrangements. These disclosures will help us to better understand the two biggest listed resources companies in Australia, BHP Billiton and Rio Tinto.

THE CASE OF BHP BILLITON

Overview

Incorporated in 1885, BHP was one of the oldest companies in Australia (BHP Billiton, 2004a). BHP was merged with Billiton in 2001 and became the world's largest diversified resources company. In 2001, BHP Billiton was roughly 70% bigger than the next biggest player in its sector, Rio Tinto (Bartholomeusz, 2001). According to the top 500 companies list published by *Business Review Weekly*, BHP Billiton was the biggest listed company in Australia in terms of market capitalization in 2002 and 2003 (Baker et al., 2002; Baker et al., 2003), and the second biggest in 2004[1] (Ng et al., 2004). In 2004, BHP Billiton employed about 35,000 people and its operations expanded across 20 countries (BHP Billiton, 2004a). In 2008, BHP Billiton's number of employees grew to 39,000 people with its 100 operations spread across 25 countries (BHP Billiton, 2008). BHP Billiton's headquarters is located in Melbourne, Australia.

BHP Billiton is also a dual-listed company (DLC). As the Australian Secruities and Investments Commission (ASIC) has noted, a dual-listed company (DLC) structure:

> . . . involves two companies contractually agreeing to operate their businesses as if they were a unified enterprise, while retaining their separate legal identity and existing Stock Exchange listings. (ASIC, 2004)

In BHP Billiton's case, BHP Billiton Ltd. and BHP Billiton plc are respectively listed on the ASX and the London Stock Exchange.

DLC and Possible Governance Issues at BHP Billiton

BHP Billiton's DLC structure suggests that if another company launches a takeover bid for one company in the DLC structure, it will also trigger a bid on proportional terms for the other company (ASIC, 2004). Because both BHP and Billiton were already very big companies, the merger of the two has made BHP Billiton a massive company, which makes it a very difficult, if not impossible, takeover target. In terms of governance concerns, the takeover market is one external mechanism that may operate to discipline a company's board and its management team. However, the DLC structure in effect "weakens the position of shareholders and entrenches the position of board and management" (Hulme cited in Kemp, 2003: 1). But, this is also the case in many large listed companies with a widely dispersed shareholding, as legal scholars have long pointed out (Eisenberg, 1976).

Arguably, the DLC structure may also weaken the legal system of a country. As Hulme has suggested:

> To enable the BHP Billiton DLC structure to be adopted in Australia, [ASIC] gave dispensations with respect to not less than 160 provisions of the Corporations Act. (cited in Kemp, 2003: 1)

However, the DLC structure may also provide greater transparency. The fact that the company has to comply with the highest standards in the disclosure requirements of different jurisdictions suggests that there may be greater transparency in terms of the disclosure of its corporate governance practices and mechanisms.

Historical Governance Issue Highlighted in BHP Billiton—the Beswick Deal

In the governance history of BHP Billiton, one event that attracted much public attention in Australia was the long takeover battle for BHP led by Robert Holmes à Court in the mid-1980s (Haigh, 1987). In 1988, Beswick was established by BHP as a takeover defense, after Robert Holmes à Court's attack on BHP.

BHP became a takeover target in the 1980s due to the fact that its share price was well below what might be expected from a review of its net tangible assets (Sykes, 1994: 413). The Beswick deal was structured in such a way that BHP held about 50% of the ordinary shares of Beswick, Elders IXL (now Fosters Brewing) held 49.999% and ANZ Executors & Agency held 0.001% (Frith, 1997). BHP's effective ownership of Beswick increased to 97.3% after taking into account the preference shares that it held (Smith, 1998). In return, Beswick owned about 18% of BHP, which effectively "created a structure (to enable BHP) to own a significant slice of itself" (McIlwraith, 1993). This type of arrangement "not only [served] as a formidable takeover defense, but also [acted] as a powerful means of entrenching the board and management" (Frith, 1998). The 18% voting shares held by Beswick effectively meant that BHP could vote for itself. In 1994, a request made by the Australian Shareholders Association (ASA) for BHP to cancel the 18% voting rights in BHP held by Beswick (Kaye, 1994) was unsuccessful. In the same year, BHP was able to avoid the Beswick deal being categorized (by the Australian Securities Commission [ASC]) as an "unacceptable self-acquisition" (Frith, 1998).

The heavy losses suffered by BHP in 1997 and 1998 led some shareholders to argue that the shares held by Beswick made the board less accountable than they otherwise may have been for the performance of BHP (Ernst & Young quoted in Wood, 1999). This criticism probably contributed to the ending of the controversial Beswick deal in 1999. During March 1999, BHP entered into an agreement to buy back shares held by Beswick in four separate tranches (BHP Billiton, 2001). With the buyback of Beswick's shares in 1999, BHP started to adopt a more transparent share structure. In hindsight, the construction of the Beswick deal as a takeover defense by seeking to exploit voting rights was a flawed corporate governance practice, as it challenged the transparency of these practices.

Corporate Governance Structure at BHP Billiton

Corporate governance practices in BHP Billiton have changed dramatically since the controversies raised by the Beswick deal. According to one report, the corporate governance structure of BHP Billiton subsequently was seen as outstanding, at least in terms of *director independence, structure of board committees* and *audit independence*; this conclusion was based on the information disclosed in its 2002 annual report (Psaros, 2003). In 2004, BHP Billiton also won the Corporate Governance Reporting Award and the Occupational Health and Safety Reporting Award, administered by the Australasian Reporting Awards (The Australian, 2004b). In 2007, BHP Billiton was again the Gold Award Winner of the Australasian Reporting Awards, which were originally established in 1951 and sought to improve reporting to stakeholders (BHP Billiton, 2007a).

The DLC status of BHP Billiton may help to improve the corporate governance practices of the group, as DLCs need to comply with the higher governance test in the two different jurisdictions (Duris, 2004). In BHP Billiton's case, the company issued two annual reports each year to comply with the different disclosure requirements of Australia and the UK. Since the two annual reports are effectively reporting on the same group, the two reports will be evaluated together to help to draw a more comprehensive picture of corporate governance practices in BHP Billiton. Because BHP Billitons' shares are traded in the US as American Depository Receipts (ADRs), the company also needs to comply with corporate governance requirements in the US. Overall, the company needs to comply with the following listing rules and requirements (BHP Billiton, 2007c: 142):

1. The Listing Rules of the UK Listing Authority require reporting on the extent to which a listed company has complied with its Principles of Good Governance and Code of Best Practice, which are contained in Section 1 of the Combined Code of Corporate Governance.
2. The Listing Rules of the ASX require reporting on the extent that the company has met the Principles of Good Corporate Governance issued by the Australian Corporate Governance Council.
3. The Sarbanes-Oxley Act (US) and regulations made by the Securities and Exchange Commission.

The degree of compliance by BHP Billiton with these regulations and corporate governance codes was set out in the company's 2007 annual report. An overview of the corporate goverance structure in BHP Billiton is illustrated in Figure 5.1.

The corporate governance model shown in Figure 5.1 illustrates that BHP Billiton's board of directors appoints and monitors the CEO and that the CEO is accountable to the board for the overall management and operations of the company. Also, the board has established various sub-committees, such as a risk and audit committee, a sustainability committee, a nomination committee and a remuneration committee to assist it (BHP Billiton, 2007c: 136); the board also provides oversight of external auditors; group audit services; health, safety, environment and community (HSEC)

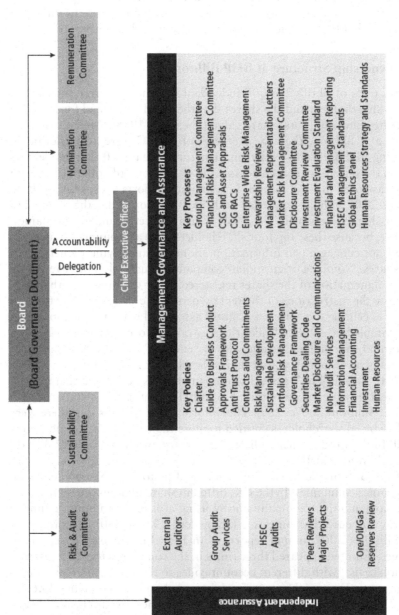

Figure 5.1 BHP Billiton governance assurance diagram. Source: *BHP Billiton annual report 2007* (BHP Billiton, 2007c: 131).

audits; peer review of major projects; and an ore, oil and gas review. On the other hand, the CEO is responsible for establishing proper policies and maintaining the functions of management committees as illustrated in Figure 5.1. In summary, the corporate governance structure in BHP Billiton is fairly typical of the so-called Anglo-American model of governance.

The Ownership Structure at BHP Billiton

In 1998, 60% of BHP's 285,000 individual shareholders were categorized as small shareholders and the shares that they held accounted for less than 4% of the company's total share value (Pheasant, 1998). After the merger of BHP and Billiton, the characteristics of a DLC were also relevant in evaluating BHP Billiton's ownership structure. The top 20 shareholders (as listed on the register of shareholders) of BHP Billiton Ltd. and BHP Billiton plc are disclosed in BHP Billiton Ltd.'s annual reports. According to BHP Billiton's 2007 annual report (as with BHP Billiton Ltd.), the company's top four shareholders held 45.13% of shares registered under their names. However, because these top four shareholders were all nominee companies, this did not convey much information about the underlying ownership of these shares. Nominee or custodian companies usually do not have voting rights in aggregation of the shares registered under their names—they simply follow the instructions of the real owners of the shares held by them in terms of executing the "property rights" associated with the corresponding shares (Stapledon, 1996a). Under the Australian Corporations Act 2001, a "substantial shareholder" is one who is "entitled" to not less than 5% of any class of a company's voting shares (Stapledon, 1996a: 329).

In BHP Billiton Ltd.'s case, the company has also disclosed that no person beneficially owned more than 5% of BHP Billiton Ltd.'s voting securities (BHP Billiton, 2007c: 289). This information indicates that there were no substancial shareholders entitled to more than 5% of the voting shares in BHP Billiton Ltd., which indicates that share ownership in BHP Billiton Ltd. is relatively widely dispersed.

In BHP Billiton plc's case, the majority of its top 20 shareholders were also nominee companies. In the UK, different shareholdings are represented by the same nominee company but by using a different in-house nominee company for custodial purposes (Stapledon, 1996a: 330). According to BHP Billiton's 2007 annual report, as in BHP Billiton plc's case, Chase Nominees Limited appeared three times in the company's top 20 registered shareholder list, with different account codes to represent different ownership interests. Despite the top two registered shareholders having 23.66% and 4.57% of shares, respectively, under their names, the disclosure of substantial shareholders indicated a different picture. According to the UK's listing requirements, a shareholder who owns 3% or more of a company is characterized as a substantial shareholder. In the case of BHP Billiton plc, there were two substantial shareholders, holding 4.82% and 3.53%.

None of these substantial shareholders were listed in list of the top 20 registered shareholders. Altogether, two substantial shareholders held 8.35% of the total shares in the company. This indicates that the overall ownership structure in the BHP Billiton Group was relatively widely held.

Board Composition and the Function of Board Committees at BHP Billiton

Another important indicator of the nature of corporate governance is the composition of a company's board. Although BHP Billiton is a DLC, BHP Billiton Ltd. and BHP Billiton plc have identical boards of directors and are run by a unified management team (BHP Billiton, 2004b). The board composition of BHP Billiton will be reviewed in the following section.

The composition of the BHP Billiton board, as disclosed in the company's 2007 annual report, indicates that there were 12 directors and that 60% of directors have served more than three years; among these directors, half have actually served for more than nine years. One benefit of this situation could be that BHP Billiton directors not only understood the company's business, but that they also understood each other in terms of working as a whole group; on the other hand, a criticism that might be made is that the board members were too entrenched to play an independent role.

According to the BHP Billiton 2007 annual report:

> An appropriate balance between executive and non-executive directors is necessary to promote shareholder interests and to govern the business effectively . . . [and the company should] ensure that a majority of directors are independent. (BHP Billiton, 2007c: 133)

The independence of directors is taken to mean that directors should be:

> . . . independent of management and any business or other relationship that could materially interfere with the exercise of objective, unfettered or independent judgement by the director or the director's ability to act in the best interests of the BHP Billiton Group. (BHP Billiton, 2007c: 133)

The number of independent directors on a company's board usually indicates the level of board independence. In the case of BHP Billiton, as noted in its 2007 annual report, of its 12 board members, ten were independent non-executive directors, two were executive directors and the chairman of the board was an independent non-executive director.

In terms of its board committees, the 2007 BHP Billiton annual report disclosed that the company has set up a remuneration committee under its board and that all the members of the remuneration committee are independent non-executive directors (BHP Billiton, 2007c). The company's

2007 annual report also disclosed remuneration details for its directors and senior executives.

In regard to the functions of BHP Billiton Group's risk and audit committee, this includes "assisting the board in monitoring decisions and actions of the CEO and the Group and providing assurance that progress is being made towards the Corporate Objective within the CEO's limit" (BHP Billiton, 2007c: 137). To facilitate its work, separate risk and audit committees have also been established in each Customer Services Group (CSG) and key functional areas of BHP Billiton (BHP Billiton, 2007c: 137). The company's risk and audit committee is composed of four independent non-executive directors.

The major role of BHP Billiton's nomination committee is to assess the skill levels needed for the company's board and to nominate approporiate candidates to the board, in order to ensure proper governance within the board. The board also has a sustainability committee which is tasked with overseeing HSEC matters across the group (BHP Billiton, 2007c: 139). Given BHP Billiton's strong commitment to health, safety, environmental and commnity (HSEC) issues,[2] it is not surprising to find that a specific board committee has been set up to deal wih this area. BHP started to issue its environmental reports in 1997 and this evolved to become the HSEC report, and in 2005, the HSEC report was renamed the Sustainability Report.

Disclosure of Related Party Transactions at BHP Billiton

According to its 2007 annual report, the company had an *effective* full-ownership interest in 61 subsidiaries and held controlling interests (of more than 50%) in nine other subsidiaries (BHP Billiton, 2007c: 252–253). The sheer size of BHP Billiton and the complexity of its operational arrangements and subsidiary arrangements gives rise to the issue of related party transactions. The company's annual report indicates that BHP Billiton has complied with legal disclosure requirements and that its related party transactions were conducted on a fully competitive basis and were not used to disadvantage any shareholder interests.

Other Stakeholders and Corporate Governance in BHP Billiton

Apart from the governance issues just discussed, stakeholder roles in corporate governance are another important issue in corporate governance. Before we explore the stakeholders' role in corporate governance in BHP Billiton, its major stakeholders need to be defined.

As illustrated in BHP Billiton's 2007 sustainability report (BHP Billiton, 2007b), the company saw its major global stakeholders as being its employees and contractors, local and indigenous communities, shareholders, customers, the investment community, business partners, community organizations, unions, non-government organizations, suppliers, governments (including regulators), media and industry associations. The role of major stakeholders in corporate governance is discussed further in the following paragraphs.

The role of employees in corporate governance has two aspects. First, there is the question of whether employees' interests have been considered in the governance of the corporation, for example, whether the company has provided a safe working environment for its employees and whether the social and economic benefits of employees are considered to contribute to the better governance of the company. Second, apart from the passive role of employees in corporate governance, there is the question of whether employees have actively participated in governing the company; for example, whether employee representatives are appointed to the board. In countries such as Germany and Japan where corporate governance models are characterized as insider-based, employees are normally involved in electing board members as well as either directly or indirectly making other major decisions of the company. This is part of the system of "co-determination," as it is described in Germany.

In its 2007 sustainability report, BHP Billiton extensively documented its health, safety and socio-economic management policy in terms of the health and well-being of its employees. Apart from maintaining a safe working environment and providing personal protective equipment to employees, BHP Billiton has also reported on how the social and economic interests of its employees are managed. For example, one of the main areas of social and economic interest of employees includes freedom of association, where employees have the right to join trade unions. BHP Billiton also seeks to help employees achieve a work and life balance and to provide fair remuneration. However, there is no evidence of employees participating directly in corporate governance, such as by being appointed as board members, which is typical in the insider-based model. However, superannuation funds (pension funds) into which BHP Billiton employees contribute would be expected to hold BHP Billiton shares as part of their investment portfolios.

The most publicized corporate governance role of unions that operate within BHP has concerned whether each employee should have an individually negotiated contract (Kohler, 2001). It seemed that the union's role in BHP Billiton was less far reaching than that of unions in Rio Tinto; in 2000, the Rio Tinto unions called for changes at the board level so as to increase the power of non-executive directors (Long, 2000c: 24); this matter is further discussed later in the case study of Rio Tinto.

In BHP Billiton, the union was actively involved in forming coalitions with institutional investors to fight against the 2001 merger between BHP and Billiton. This action was taken because the union believed that the merger was bad for shareholders as well as for the company's workers (Long and Oldfield, 2001; Callick, 2001).

According to BHP Billiton's 2007 sustainability report, managing relationships with different stakeholders is intertwined with the four major perspectives of sustainability: health, safety, environment and community. Moreover, the economic interests of shareholders and stakeholders in the area of health, safety and environment also need to be taken care of. The long-term economic interests of the company and its shareholders cannot be advanced without proper management of stakeholders' interests in terms of health, safety, environment and community (BHP Billiton, 2007b). BHP Billiton's commitment to the interests of its stakeholders in terms of health, safety, environmental responsibility and sustainable development is also embedded in the company's vision and values. As the company has said:

> Our vision for sustainable development is to be the company of choice—creating sustainable value for shareholders, employees, contractors, suppliers, customers, business partners and host communities. Central to our vision is our aspirational goal of Zero Harm to people, our host communities and the environment. (BHP Billiton, 2007b: 40)

BHP Billiton's performance in achieving these goals is reflected in its inclusion in various market indexes:

- The Dow Jones Sustainability World Indexes (DJSI), which selects the top 10% of the leading sustainability companies in 60 industry groups in the 34 countries covered by the biggest 2500 companies in the Dow Jones Global Indexes (BHP Billiton, 2007b: 25).
- The FTSE4Good index, which is designed to facilitate investment in companies that meet globally recognized corporate responsibility standards (BHP Billiton, 2007b: 25).
- The Australian SAM Sustainability Index, which tracks the performance of Australian companies that lead their industry in terms of corporate sustainability (BHP Billiton, 2007b: 25).
- The 2006 Climate Leadership Index of the Carbon Disclosure Project, and Johannesburg Stock Exchange Socially Responsible Investment Index (BHP Billiton, 2007b).

In 2003, RepuTex, an independent rating agency, gave BHP Billiton an AA rating (the highest being AAA, the lowest being D), in the area of social responsibility, which includes criteria such as environment, social impact and workplace practices[3] (RepuTex, 2003). In 2007, the company was also among the highest ranked companies in terms of its reputation based on media coverage of the company (Insiderinvestment, 2008).

One of the major concerns of corporate governance relates to local communities being involved in environmental issues. BHP Billiton detailed its environmental performance in its 2007 sustainability report. Major areas covered there included environmental incidents and fines, environmental spending, closure, biodiversity, resource use, waste and emissions (BHP Billiton, 2007b: 205–219). BHP Billiton is also ISO 14001 certified (BHP

Billiton, 2007b: 2), which in a way illustrates that BHP Billiton is committed to continuous improvement in the areas of environmental management.[4] However, as we will see below, BHP Billiton's poor handling of its community relations in OK Tedi in Papua New Guinea led to considerable controversy and the eventual withdrawal of the company from these mining operations.

The Case of Ok Tedi

Some of the most controversial issues relating to BHP Billiton's corporate governance in terms of environmental management were demonstrated in the Ok Tedi case. Ok Tedi was a mining site operated by BHP Billiton in Papua New Guinea (PNG) until 2002.

The mining practices of BHP Billiton at Ok Tedi were seriously challenged by local communities in PNG. The environmental damage that occurred at Ok Tedi was well documented by Tilburn (2002). Not only did BHP Billiton dump tailings directly into the Ok Tedi river—a practice outlawed in the US and Australia many years earlier (Kennedy, 1996)—it also attempted to strip away local landowner rights (Imhof, 1996: 16). In 1995, BHP "helped draft a bill which eliminated the rights of PNG citizens adversely affected by the mine to seek compensation in court" (Imhof, 1996: 15).

The controversy over environmental issues at Ok Tedi lasted for some years. In 2002, BHP Billiton set up Papua New Guinea Sustainable Development Program Ltd. (PNGSDP). BHP Billiton's 52% share of equity at Ok Tedi was transferred to PNGSDP (BHP Billiton, 2004c: 124), and the dividend from Ok Tedi would be paid into PNGSDP (BHP Billiton, 2004c: 124). The main aim of PNGSDP was to make contributions to the community that had been so adversely affected by its mining operations at Ok Tedi. However, from another perspective, this was perceived as a negative result, as it had insulated BHP from further lawsuits in relation to Ok Tedi. As Burton wrote:

> . . . the Papua New Guinea (PNG) government has passed legislation that prevents any government agency from taking or supporting "in any way" proceedings against the mining multinational BHP Billiton "in respect of an environmental claim" over damage caused by the Ok Tedi mine. (Burton, 2002: 6)

This PNG legislation also put in effect another agreement which forfeited rights to sue BHP Billiton at a future date (Burton, 2002). This infuriated some of the local residents of Ok Tedi. As one landowner commented, "If we let BHP walk away from its environmental and social responsibilities now, Papua New Guinea will come to regret this decision forever" (Burton, 2002: 6).

On the other hand, a BHP company spokesman admitted that Ok Tedi had "taught the company a lesson" (Horstman, 1997: 6). He also made the following comments:

We got some things wrong . . . We don't want to do them again . . . We think we will pay more attention [to environmental and indigenous rights issues] than most companies, not the reverse. (Horstman, 1997: 6)

The controversial Ok Tedi case illustrates how major activities of multinational companies have already expanded well beyond national boundaries. As a consequence, a company's treatment of stakeholders in its operational sites should also be included when evaluating its overall corporate governance polices and practices.

Summary

In 2002, BHP Billiton's corporate governance structure was seen as being outstanding in the Horwath Report (Psaros and Seamer, 2002); the analysis in this chapter supports the conclusion that overall, BHP Billiton has an outstanding corporate governance structure. The general level of information disclosed by BHP Billiton can be categorized as extensive. The information disclosed in BHP Billiton's 2007 annual report and in its 2007 sustainability report is adequate and comprehensive.

In general, BHP Billiton is a typical company with an outsider-based corporate governance model. Its board is dominated by independent directors and board sub-committees are also established within the board to deal with specific governance issues. But, other stakeholders, and especially its employees, have played a somewhat passive role in corporate governance, as is generally the case in companies with an outsider-based corporate governance model.

The Case of Rio Tinto

Like BHP Billiton, Rio Tinto is also one of the world's leading miners; its history can be traced back to 1873, when Rio Tinto Company was formed to undertake mining work in Spain (Rio Tinto, 2004a). The current Rio Tinto Group was created by the 1995 merger of Conzinc Riotinto of Australia (CRA), the Melbourne-based miner, and Britain's Rio Tinto-Zinc Corporation (RTZ); it became a dual-listed company (The Australian, 2004a). Rio Tinto plc and Rio Tinto Ltd. are, respectively, listed on the London Stock Exchange and the ASX. Rio Tinto is such a big company that at one stage "four of the top seven companies listed on the Melbourne Stock Exchange were subsidiaries of RTZ" (West, 1974).

In 2004, the company employed about 36,000 employees on 70 sites in 40 countries (Ashworth, 2004). In 2004, Rio Tinto ranked fifth on the top 500 public companies list published by the *Business Review Weekly* (Ng et al., 2004). On June 5, 2008, Rio Tinto's market capitalization was AUS$64 billion and it ranked third on the Australian top 100 companies list (The Australian, 2008). According to Rio Tinto's 2007 annual report, Rio Tinto is a leading international mining group, with its business focusing on finding, mining and processing mineral resources (Rio Tinto, 2007). Rio Tinto's management structure is organized around its six major product groups, namely, aluminum, diamonds, copper, energy (coal and uranium), industrial minerals and iron ore (Rio Tinto, 2008c). In 2007, the company was also among the highest ranked in terms of its reputation, based on media coverage of the company (Insiderinvestment, 2008).

The Corporate Governance Structure of Rio Tinto

In the area of corporate governance, the Rio Tinto Group complied with the Combined Code of Corporate Governance, published by the UK Financial Reporting Council, and with the ASX's Corporate Governance Council Principles and Recommendations (Rio Tinto, 2008c). According to an investor poll conducted by *Asianmoney*, Rio Tinto was ranked first as the best-managed company in terms of economic performance as well as for its corporate governance and general management (Keri, 2004).

Despite the fact that Rio Tinto is a DLC, the company group operates as a single business entity with the same board of directors and a unified management team (Rio Tinto, 2007). Its corporate governance structure is illustrated in Figure 5.2.

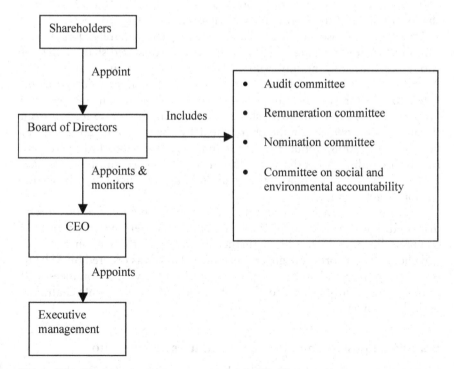

Figure 5.2 Corporate governance structure in Rio Tinto.

As illustrated in Figure 5.2, the corporate governance model found in Rio Tinto is similar to that in BHP Billiton. Rio Tinto established four committees under its board, namely, an audit committee, a remuneration committee, a nomination committee and a committee on social and environmental accountability. The major functions of these board committees are reviewed in a following section.

The Ownership Structure at Rio Tinto

The company disclosed its substantial shareholders in its 2007 annual report. In Rio Tinto plc's case, the substantial shareholders were Barclays plc, The Capital Group Companies, Legal & General plc, AXA S.A. and Shining Prospect Pte. Ltd. These shareholders accounted for more than 18% of the shares in Rio Tinto plc. In the case of Rio Tinto Limited, there were two substantial shareholders, i.e., Shining Prospect Pte. Ltd. and Alcoa Inc.; the amount of shares held by these two shareholders was undisclosed.

In addition, Rio Tinto disclosed other statistical information in bands about its shareholders, such as the number of shareholders that held between one and 1,000 shares, and from 1,001 to 5,000 shares, 5,001 to 10,000 shares, 10,001 to 25,000 shares, 25,001 to 125,000 shares, 125,001 to 250,000 shares, 250,001 to 1,250,000 shares, 1,250,001 to 2,500,000 shares and 2,500,001 shares and over (Rio Tinto, 2007: 131).

The company also disclosed the top 20 registered shareholders of Rio Tinto Ltd. As of February 22, 2008, the top 20 registered shareholders of Rio Tinto Ltd. were mainly nominee companies (Rio Tinto, 2007: 131). As with BHP Billiton, the Rio Tinto nominee companies held shares on behalf of their respective clients. Nominee companies can only execute property rights associated with shares based on instructions received from the underlying owners of the shares held by them (Dolin, 2002). As of February 22, 2008, about 37.45% of shares in Rio Tinto Ltd. were held by Tinto Holding Australia Pty. Ltd.—a wholly owned subsidiary of Rio Tinto plc. This type of quasi-cross-shareholding has huge implications for corporate governance.[5]

Only on rare occasions would the real owners of nominee companies be disclosed. For example, in 2000, in the battle between the union and the company board (which will be further discussed in the section on other stakeholders and corporate governance), Rio Tinto was ordered by ASIC to reveal the names and addresses of organizations for whom nominees held shares (Long, 2000b), so as to allow the union to form possible coalitions with shareholder activists (Long, 2000b).

Board Composition and Board Committees at Rio Tinto

In Australia in 2000, the Rio Tinto board was seen as "one of the worst boards" (Kohler, 2000), as half of its board members were executives; the chairman of the board was also an executive and the former CEO was appointed to the board as a non-executive director (Kohler, 2000). It was not until 2003 that the role of the CEO and the chairman started to be separated at Rio Tinto (FitzGerald, 2003). In 2008, the company had three executive directors (including the CEO) and seven non-excutive directors. The chairman of the board is a non-executive director (Rio Tinto, 2008a). However, the company had not distinguished between its non-executive directors and independent directors.

Of the four committees under the board, the role of the remuneration committee is to:

- recommend executive remuneration policy to the board;
- review and determine the remuneration packages of the executive directors, product group chief executives and the company secretary of Rio Tinto plc;
- review and agree to the remuneration strategy and conditions of employment for managers other than the executives;
- monitor the effectiveness and appropriateness of the company's general executive remuneration policy and practice; and
- review the chairman's fees (Rio Tinto, 2007: 103).

The functions of other board sub-committees were also covered in the company's 2007 annual report; this especially dealt with the role of the committee for social and environmental accountability, which aims to ensure that there are policies, standards, systems and people in place to meet the company's social and environmental commitments; its role is also to ensure that the company's businesses, projects, operations and products are developed and implemented in line with its commitment to sustainable development (Rio Tinto, 2007: 83).

The Rio Tinto Group's Structure and Its Governance Implications

To help us understand governance issues at Rio Tinto, the company's corporate structure also needs to be reviewed. In 2008, the company's operations were mainly located in Australia, North America, South America, Asia, Europe and Southern Africa, with its major products including aluminum, copper, diamonds, energy products, gold, industrial minerals (borates, titanium dioxide, salt and talc) and iron ore (Rio Tinto, 2008d). As listed in Rio Tinto's 2007 financial report, Rio Tinto had 57 subsidiaries (Rio Tinto, 2008e). The complexity of Rio Tinto's group structure inevitably complicates its governance arrangements.

Disclosure of Related Party Transactions by Rio Tinto

In Rio Tinto's 2007 annual report and financial report, the company provided detailed disclosures of its investments in subsidiaries and related party transactions. The thorough disclosure of related party transactions can arguably help to minimize unfair related party transactions.

Other Stakeholder Roles in Corporate Governance and Environmental Issues at Rio Tinto

The major stakeholders of Rio Tinto need to be reviewed before those stakeholder roles in corporate governance are analyzed. Because of the diversity of its operations, Rio Tinto has not provided a list of all its stakeholders in its group level report. Each operation has instead identified its own stakeholders in its local, social and environment report according to the characteristics of its operations.[6]

In 2003, the independent rating agency Reputex gave Rio Tinto an A rating in terms of its environmental impact, corporate governance, social impact and workplace practices.[7] Overall, the company's stakeholder interests were said to be managed in the following way:

> Rio Tinto conducts its affairs in an accountable and transparent manner, reflecting the interests of Rio Tinto shareholders, employees, host communities and customers as well as others affected by the Group's activities. (Rio Tinto, 2004b: 56)

In 2003, Rio Tinto also won the Australian Reporting Award (ARA), an award for its accountability and disclosure practices, with an emphasis on corporate social responsibility (Kaye, 2003).

One of the characteristics of the mining industry is that big mining companies generally operate globally. In Rio Tinto's case, because of the diversity of its stakeholders in its different operations, each subsidiary publishes its own social and environment report (Rio Tinto, 2003c). In 1999, only ten operations issued their individual social and environmental reports, with the number increasing to 24 in 2000. In each year from 2001 to 2003, 31 Rio Tinto operations each year issued their own social and environmental reports[8] and these operations continued to follow this strategy in their sustainability reporting in 2007. It was also declared on the company's website that its 2007 sustainablity review was constructed following the Global Reporting Initiative (GRI), which provides a framework for companies to report on their environmental and social performance in association with their financial performance (Global Reporting Initiative, 2008).

Turning to employee roles in corporate governance, as declared by Rio Tinto (Rio Tinto, 2008g), one of the company's major responsibilities to its employees related to occupational health. Employees were also important stakeholders of the company (Rio Tinto, 2008g). Overall, employee health and wellbeing is an integral part of Rio Tinto's responsibility to its employees, and the company's focus is on occupational health and safety.

In 2000, Rio Tinto's unions were actively involved in the company's corporate governance through their roles as institutional investors. Their major aim was to utilize the unions' role as shareholder (through their investment of superannuation funds of employees) so as to make changes to the board. The extensive media coverage given to the Rio Tinto union activities in 2000 illustrated that unions had adopted a new approach in dealing with corporate governance problems in the company. The action involved a "union coalition spanning three continents lodging proxy battles" to seek changes in corporate governance practices in the board (Burr, 2000).

On March 8, 2000, it was reported that "[Rio Tinto's] unions had forged a global alliance to try to oust the current board of mining giant Rio Tinto through an *unprecedented* strategy of shareholder activism" (Long, 2000d: 1). The focus of the union was upon "calling for changes to Rio Tinto's board structure so as to increase the power of non-executive directors" (Long, 2000c: 24). The company responded to union shareholder activism by accusing unions of trying to impose "parochial" Australian standards of corporate governance on a global company (Long, 2000a: 4). Nevertheless, this new type of 'union shareholder activism' (Long, 2000c: 24) stood in stark contrast to former union practices, such as strikes, historically used by the union.

This strategy was also perceived as something of a landmark in that the union's activities at Rio Tinto had moved from the conventional rules-oriented approach (that is, using the right to strike) to a 'Wall-Street rules' approach. As Kohler (2000) observed, the union's attempt to move a motion at a general meeting of shareholders by influencing the shareholders' meeting was indeed the "start of a new era of shareholder activism." This was due to a number of factors, including that the conventional tool of strike action had lost its power (McCarthy, 2000) and partly because the union was now able to use workers' wealth (which was tied up in the union-dominated superannuation fund) to allow employee arguments to be heard at the annual shareholder's meeting (McCarthy, 2000). An agreement was finally reached in 2001 between unions and Rio Tinto (Kohler, 2001).

Enhancing the company's "community relationship" is also treated as an important part of corporate governance at Rio Tinto. As proclaimed in Rio Tinto's 2008 Statement of Business Practices, "Good management of community relationships is as necessary to our business success as the management of our operations" (Rio Tinto, 2008g: 8).

Rio Tinto's major community-related activities also included assisting with regional development and training and providing employment and small business opportunities. In collaboration with others, Rio Tinto also seeks to help developing countries construct health, education and agricultural programs (Rio Tinto, 2008g: 8).

Environmental concerns are always an important issue for the mining industry. To achieve a high standard of environment protection in its operational sites, Rio Tinto has declared the following environmental policy:

"Wherever possible we prevent, or otherwise minimise, mitigate and reme-diate, harmful effects of the Group's operations on the environment" (Rio Tinto, 2008g: 9).

For example, in Coal & Allied, one of Rio Tinto's subsidiaries, environ-mental issues were broken down into several parts, such as greenhouse gas emissions, fresh water use, rehabilitation and disturbance, number of inci-dents and number of complaints (Rio Tinto, 2003b: 12). Another practice is to involve community members in environmental management, and to keep them informed about whether there would be any adverse effects of Rio Tinto's operations upon the environment and of actions that Rio Tinto was taking to minimize this (Rio Tinto, 2003a).

Since 2003, the Rio Tinto group company has also committed to reduc-ing emissions from its operations and seeking to work with supply chain partners to develop low emission products and engaging with governments and stakeholders to develop climate change policies (Rio Tinto, 2008b). Furthermore, the company was also committed to minimization, mitiga-tion and remediation of the harmful effects of its operations and products on air and water around its mines (Rio Tinto, 2008f).

However, Rio Tinto was not free from environmental controversies. His-torically, Rio Tinto-Zinc (RTZ) was "accused of polluting the environment and endangering the health of employees" (West, 1974: 76). Various com-munity disputes have involved issues in relation to industrial disputes and the environment in Rio Tinto's mines, such as in the Jabiluka uranium mine, the Bougainville copper mine, the Freeport Grasber copper mine and its Lihir gold mine (Manning, 2003). The company's decision to withdraw from its Jabiluka uranium mine in 2001 indicated that stakeholders' interests would be recognized, as well as the interests of shareholders (Rose, 2001). This withdrawal also "reflect[s] the increasing importance of stakeholders and ethical matters in corporate decision making" (Rose, 2001); these issues were raised to such a height that some even took the view that "the beginnings of a new corporate culture may have been born in Australia" (Rose, 2001).

SUMMARY

The two case studies of BHP Billiton and Rio Tinto discussed in this chap-ter illustrate that corporate governance practices and mechanisms in these two companies have largely reflected patterns found in the outsider-based model of the corporation. These included a dispersed–share ownership structure, a more developed market mechanism and other characteris-tics associated with the outsider-based model, such as the introduction of independent directors and board sub-committees aimed at alleviating the agency problem. Another feature was the relatively weak role of employees in actively participating in corporate governance in these Australian com-panies, when this is compared with union roles in Germany and Japan.

Other stakeholder roles in corporate governance were also reduced to a mere passive involvement.

To provide a fuller picture of corporate governance practices at resources industry leaders across the world, brief case studies of Shell and Chevron are also provided below. Shell and Chevron are both important players in the oil industry, with a century's history behind their well-known brand names, as well as having faced criticism of their operations worldwide (Sampson, 1975).

THE CASE OF SHELL

Overview

Royal Dutch Shell's (Shell) history can be traced back more than a century to 1890 when Royal Dutch Petroleum Company was formed to develop an oil field in Sumatra in the then Dutch East Indies (Shell, 2008c). Shell Transport and Trading Company was formed in 1897 with a focus on oil transportation (Yergin, 1993; Shell, 2008c; Howarth, 1997). In 1907, the two groups were fully integrated to become Royal Dutch Shell Group (Shell, 2008c) and the merged entity rapidly expanded across Europe and many parts of Asia (Shell, 2008c). Today the company focuses both on the upstream business of gas and power exploration and production, and the downstream businesses of oil products, chemicals and oil sands (Shell, 2008a). The company has 104,000 employees based in more than 110 countries (Shell, 2008b).

Shell was one of the first companies to become dual listed, which it did in 1903, with Royal Dutch Petroleum being listed in Amsterdam and Shell Transport and Trading being listed in London (Bedi and Tennant, 2002). The unification of the Royal Dutch and the Shell Group of companies was approved by the board in October 2004, with a belief that a single corporate strucutre would help with simplifying governance structures and improving accountability and efficiency (Shell, 2004).

Board Composition and Board Committees

As reported on Shell's website (Shell, 2008d), Shell's board is composed of 14 directors, with four executive directors and ten independent directors. The chairman of the company is an independent director. The board also has four sub-committees, including an audit committee, a nomination and succession committee, a remuneration committee and a social responsibility committee.

Sustainable Development and Shell

Despite the recent efforts of Shell to support sustainable development by becoming a member of the World Business Council for Sustainable

Development (World Business Council for Sustainable Development, 2008), Shell's environmental practices have long been criticized for not being sufficient to prevent environmental degradation in various countries, especially in developing countries (Cummins and Beasant, 2005). One of the best known cases of these crises is Shell's operation in Ogoni in Southeatern Nigeria, which has not only destroyed land, fish and wildlife resources (Cohen, 1996) but has also seen the execution of environmentalist Ken Saro-Wiwa, who led the Movement for the Survival of the Ogoni People (MOSOP) against Shell's operations there (Weissman, 1997). Furthermore, the company was criticized for trying to pay fewer royalties for using federal or tribal lands (Baldauf, 1998) and for dumping waste into the North Sea off Scotland, as it was much cheaper to do this than to dispose of it on dry land (Bandrapalli, 1996). All these actions might provide a partial explanation for the poor ranking that Shell received for its reputation, as reported recently by *Insider Investment* (Insiderinvestment, 2008).

Interestingly, Shell has been working on improving its environmental practices by employing environmentalists to critically assess the impact of its operations on the environment, a move largely viewed by observers as positive (Bakan, 2004). Recently, Shell has also tried to rebuild its image by declaring that it is also building a portfolio of alternative energy sources (other than oil), such as hydrogen, biofuels, wind power and solar power interests (Shell, 2008g). These activities need to be studied carefully to see whether they are only being used strategically to build a more positive public image for the company. Apart from publishing a comprehensive sustainability report and case studies on climate change, water conservation, environmental protection and its community relationships in the various countries in which Shell is operating (Shell, 2008e), Shell has also published a global-scenarios research paper discussing its global blueprint for energy development, including energy demand and supply, alternative energy and energy security (Shell, 2005, 2008f). Overall, these initiatives have helped Shell to build a more positive image in the marketplace, and especially in the perceptions of the general public.

THE CASE OF CHEVRON

Overview

Chevron, headquartered in San Ramon, California, is one of the top ten oil corporations in the world (Karliner, 1997) and the second-largest American oil company (Gatti and Mouawad, 2007). Over the past 130 years, Chevron has evolved from a local operator to a multinational company operating in 180 countries. In 1879, Chevron was also known as Pacific Coast Oil, which later evolved into Standard Oil Co. and Chevron Corp. Chevron's history can also be traced back to 1901, when Texas Fuel was formed in Beaumont, Texas, and it later became The Texas Co. and Texaco Inc. In 2001, Chevron Corp. and Texas Inc. merged to become Chevron Texaco. In 2005, the company changed its name to Chevron (Chevron, 2008a).

Currently, the company's 56,000 employees are based in over 180 countries. Chevron also has affiliated companies in nearly 75 countries (Chevron, 2008a). The sheer size of the company and the complexity of managing its operations in countries with vastly different social and legal frameworks continue to pose a challenge to the senior management of the company.

The high social and environmental risks associated with the oil extraction industry also contribute to the difficulty of managing the company. In the past, Chevron was much criticized for its unsound environmental management practices (Karliner, 1997). Chevron has also been criticized for its bad human rights record in Nigeria and for its irresponsibility toward communities in Angola (Karliner, 1997).

Unlike BHP Billiton and Rio Tinto, Chevron has not disclosed the names of its top shareholders.

Board Composition and Corporate Governance

The board of Chevron comprises 14 members, of which two are executive directors and 12 are independent directors (Chevron, 2008b). The governance structure of Chevron is set out in Figure 5.3.

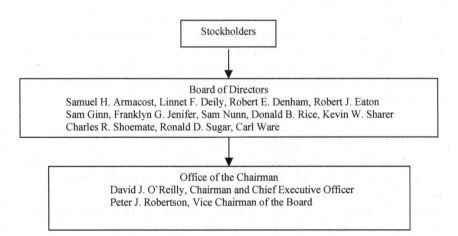

Figure 5.3 Board composition at Chevron (updated March 2008). Source: adapted from http://www.chevron.com/about/leadership/organizationchart/.

Table 5.1   Board Committees and Management Committees at Chevron

Committees of the Board	Committees Under the Executive Committee
Audit Committee (Charles R. Shoemate, chair)	Compliance Policy Committee (Peter J. Robertson, chair)
Board Nominating and Governance Committee (Samuel H. Armacost, chair)	Global Issues Committee (Peter J. Robertson, chair)
Management Compensation Committee (Robert J. Eaton, chair)	Human Resources Committee (Peter J. Robertson, chair)
Public Policy Committee (Sam Nunn, chair)	Management Committee (David J. O'Reilly, chair)
	Strategy and Planning Committee (David J. O'Reilly, chair)

Note: updated January 2008.
Source: adapted from http://www.chevron.com/about/leadership/organizationchart/.

While the board of Chevron is mainly composed of independent directors, the chairman of its board is also the CEO of Chevron. This is quite different from Anglo-Australian practice, as we have seen in cases of BHP Billiton and Rio Tinto, where the positions of CEO and the chairman of the board are clearly separated, following *Corporate Governance Principles and Recommendations*, issued by the ASX Corporate Governance Council (ASX Corporate Governance Council, 2007) and following the UK Combined Code of Corporate Governance.

Chevron's board committees and other committees under the executive committee are illustrated in Table 5.1.

As shown in Table 5.1, Chevron has four committees directly under its board. They are: (i) an audit committee, (ii) a board nominating and governance committee, (iii) a management compensation committee and (iv) a public policy committee. All these committees are chaired by independent directors. There are also five committees under the company's executive committee whose main responsibility is to manage the company.

Environmental Issues

The oil industry has widely been accused of directly or indirectly causing environmental damage (through the extractive nature of its business), air pollution (burning of fossil fuel) and global warming (Yergin, 1993). As one of the largest oil companies, Chevron's environmental management record has also been less than satisfactory.

In the past, Chevron has had a poor environmental record, with its operations causing ecological destruction around the world. As the instigator of one of the best-known environmental disasters, Chevron dumped 18.5 billion gallons of highly toxic waste into the Ecuadoran rainforest from 1970 to 1992. This was also known as the "Rainforest Chernobyl" (ChevronToxico, 2005). Chevron's toxic spill in Nigeria has also caused severe environmental damage to that region (Karliner, 1997). Furthermore, Chevron has employed different environmental standards in the US and abroad. While its operations took it to more than 100 countries outside the US, its overall environmental spending in other countries was far less than the amount spent on this area in the US (Karliner, 1997).

Ironically, despite its poor environmental record, Chevron was one of the first oil companies that established a centralized environmental policy and to adopt a commitment to reducing land toxicity (Stanford, 2000). Since 2005, the management of the company has tried to promote better environmental practices. The change to its name was also perceived as one way to improve a reputation that had been associated with unsound environmental management. Despite this history, in 2007 the company was still said to be among the companies with the worst ranking on one reputation index, as reported by Covalence Ethical Ranking, based on media coverage (Insiderinvestment, 2008).

Stakeholder Management

As stated in the company's corporate responsibility report, in 2006 Chevron employed environmental, social and health impact assessments (ESHIA) and further integrated stakeholders into its decisionmaking process (Chevron, 2007). In this report, the company also acknowledged a number of constituencies as major stakeholders of the company; they are stockholders, employees, suppliers, governments, customers, local communities and non-governmental organizations. Chevron has detailed its engagements with various stakeholders in its 2006 corporate responsibility report (Chevron, 2007: 17).

One of the major concerns for extractive industries is that payments made to governments of resource-rich countries are not always transparent. Chevron supports greater transparency in the industry by participating in the Extractive Industries Transparency Initiative (EITI) as a member of EITI's International Advisory Group (IAG) (Chevron, 2007: 16). Chevron also took the initiative and became the first company to make a substantial donation (US$30 million) to the Global Fund to Fight Aids, Tuberculosis and Malaria in countries where they operate, mainly in Asia and Africa (The Global Fund, 2008). Overall, depite its unsatisfactory environmental record and its negative image, the company has made an effort to participate in various community programs so as to contribute to the societies in which it operates. It could be said that such efforts are largely public relations driven, but that would be to oversimplify the problems faced by such industries.

SUMMARY

This chapter has presented longer case studies of global resources companies BHP Billiton and Rio Tinto and briefer case studies on Shell and Chevron. It has illustrated that apart from general corporate governance issues such as board composition and operation, resources companies are facing increasing challenges on broader governance issues, such as managing stakeholder interests and concerns, including the health and safety of employees, environmental protection and community development.

The challenges facing these companies are generally associated with the fact that resources companies are operating in industries with high risks in regard to both safety and environmental matters. Managing stakeholders' interests will pose a further challenge given deteriorating environmental conditions (ecological degradation) worldwide, which could be attributed to the extractive nature of resources exploration and broader climate change issues (such as global warming) that are associated with energy companies such as mining and oil companies.

The four case studies covered in this chapter will serve to provide comparisons with leading resources companies in China; this will help us better understand broader corporate governance issues in those Chinese companies given their growing status and their influence around the world both in terms of their economic power and their possible negative effect on environmental issues and climate change.

6 Corporate Governance in Leading Chinese Resources Companies
The Cases of Sinopec and Baosteel

How do the corporate governance practices of leading Chinese companies compare with those of industry leaders across the world? Further exploration in this chapter of governance practices in two leading Chinese resources companies, Sinopec and Baosteel, will provide some insights to allow us to answer these questions.

THE CASE OF CHINA PETROLEUM & CHEMICAL CORPORATION (SINOPEC CORP.)

Since 2001, China Petroleum & Chemical Corporation (also called Sinopec) remained at the top position in the list of China's top 100 companies published by *Fortune* magazine. In 2004, Sinopec Corp.'s revenue reached RMB ¥ 417.2 billion, which was roughly equal to AUS$69.6 billion,[1] four times higher than the revenue of Australia's diversified resources giant BHP Billiton. In 2007, its revenue jumped to US$131.6 billion and ranked number 17 on the Fortune Global 500 list (CNNMoney.com, 2008). Sinopec is listed on the Hong Kong, London, New York and the Shanghai Stock Exchanges.[2]

The History of Sinopec

The evolving history of Sinopec is closely related to the history of economic and enterprise reform in China. In fact, the development of China's stock market and listed companies (especially for those that were transformed from state-owned enterprises [SOEs]) is also closely related to economic and enterprise reform. Under the planned economy, different ministries of China not only executed the functions of the public sector but also carried out the functions normally performed by the private sector in countries with market economies.

For example, before the enterprise reforms, a typical ministry would also directly manage the operations of enterprises it was supposed to regulate. The Chinese government was well aware of this problem and it was officially known as *zhengqi bufen* (without a clear line between the management of the government and the management of enterprises). One of the main aims of economic and enterprise reform was to resolve this problem and to separate the government functions from enterprise management (*zhengqi fenkai*). Sinopec eventually evolved into today's unique model[3] partly because of the desire of the Chinese government to push major SOEs into the market and partly due to the fact that China has taken a gradualist approach in its economic and enterprise reform process. In Sinopec's case, there exists a dominant shareholder—Sinopec Group—which is an SOE. The development of the Sinopec Group and Sinopec is reviewed here.

The Sinopec Group Company originated from the China National Petrochemical Corporation (CNPC). CNPC was created in 1983 by combining refining and petrochemical assets from the then Ministry of Petroleum Industry with the chemical and synthetic-fiber manufacturing enterprises from the Ministry of Chemical Industry and the Ministry of Textile Industry (Zhang, 2004: 90). The newly created CNPC was a ministry-level corporation under the direct control of the State Council (Zhang, 2004: 90).

In the mid-1990s, subsequent reforms further transformed CNPC into a national holding company (Zhang, 2004: 99). In 1998, as a result of a streamlining of government functions, the governmental functions of the CNPC were further transferred to the State Bureau of Petroleum and Chemical Industry—a newly established body (Zhang, 2004: 102–104). In March 1998, China revealed its plan of establishing two "especially large" petroleum and petrochemical enterprise groups out of the Ministry of Chemical Industry and two existing petroleum and petrochemical companies[4] (Chen, 1998: B11B). In June 1998, a massive cross-institutional restructuring[5] of two major petroleum and gas companies in China resulted in the prototype of the current CNPC, which is now called Sinopec Group Company (Nolan, 2001). Sinopec Group Company is currently under the direct supervision of the State-owned Assets Supervision and Administration Commission (SASAC).

The Ownership Structure in Sinopec Corp.

Sinopec was set up on February 28, 2000 by Sinopec Group Company (Sinopec Corp., 2004c). Sinopec was listed on the Hong Kong, New York and the London Stock Exchanges in October 2000 and on the Shanghai Stock Exchange in 2001 (Sinopec Corp., 2004c). The share ownership structure in Sinopec is such that the Sinopec Group Company holds about 56.06% of Sinopec's total shares; those shares are also non-tradeable (Zhang, 2004). Despite the split share ownership structure reforms carried out since 2005, the controlling ownership of the government in Sinopec remains unchanged and is unlikely to change dramatically in the near future due to the government's clear desire to maintain tight control over major resources companies.

The top ten shareholders of Sinopec Corp. from 2001 to 2004 are listed in Tables 6.1, 6.2, 6.3 and 6.4.

Table 6.1 Top Ten Shareholders of Sinopec Corp. as of June 30, 2001

Name of company	Type of shares held	Number of shares held (1,000 shares)	Percentage of total shareholding
China Petrochemical Group Company (Sinopec Group Company)	State-owned shares	47,742,561	56.90%
HKSCC (Nominees) Limited	H shares	8,986,791	10.71%
China Development Bank	State-owned shares	8,775,570	10.46%
China Xinda Asset Management Corp.	State-owned shares	8,720,650	10.39%
ExxonMobil Far East Holdings Ltd.	H shares	3,168,529	3.78%
Shell Eastern (PTE) Ltd.	H shares	1,966,422	2.34%
BP Oil Espana S.A.	H shares	1,829,229	2.18%
China Orient Asset Management Corp.	State-owned shares	1,296,410	1.55%
China Huarong Asset Management Corp.	State-owned shares	586,760	0.7%
ABB Asea Brown Bovers Ltd.	ADS	457,307	0.55%

Source: Sinopec *Interim Report 2001* (Sinopec Corp., 2001).

Table 6.2 Top Ten Shareholders of Sinopec Corp. as of December 31, 2002

Name of company	Type of shares held	Number of shares held (1,000 shares)	Percentage of total shareholding
China Petroleum & Chemical Corporation (Sinopec Group Company)	State-owned shares	47,742,561	55.06%
HKSCC (Nominees) Limited	H shares	8,948,143	10.32%
China Development Bank	State-owned shares	8,775,570	10.12%
China Cinda Asset Management Corp.	State-owned shares	8,720,650	10.06%
ExxonMobil Far East Holdings Ltd.	H shares	3,168,529	3.65%
Shell Eastern (PTE) Ltd.	H shares	1,966,422	2.27%
BP Oil Espana S.A.	H shares	1,829,229	2.11%
China Orient Asset Management Corp.	State-owned shares	1,296,410	1.50%
Guo Tai Jun An Corp.[a]	State-owned shares	586,760	0.68%
TOPGOAL Company	H shares	339,065	0.39%

[a] Transferred from China Huarong Asset Management Corp. in April 2002.
Source: Sinopec *2002 Annual Report* (Sinopec Corp., 2003).

Table 6.3   Top Ten Shareholders of Sinopec Corp. as of December 31, 2003

Name of company	Type of shares held	Number of shares held (1,000 shares)	Percentage of total shareholding	As percentage of H shares
China Petroleum and Chemical Corporation (Sinopec Group Company)	State-owned shares	47,742,561	55.06%	N/A
HKSCC (Nominees) Limited	H shares	11,639,618	13.42%	69.36%
China Development Bank	State-owned shares	8,775,570	10.12%	N/A
China Cinda Asset Management Corp.	State-owned shares	8,720,650	10.06%	N/A
ExxonMobil Far East Holdings Ltd.	H shares	3,168,529	3.65%	18.88%
BP Oil Espana S.A.	H shares	1,829,229	2.11%	10.90%
China Orient Asset Management Corp.	State-owned shares	1,296,410	1.50%	N/A
Guo Tai Jun An Corp.	State-owned shares	597,188	0.69%	N/A
Social Security Fund Portfolio 107	A shares	72,100	0.08%	N/A
Xinghe Securities Investment Fund	A shares	61,948	0.07%	N/A

Source: Sinopec *2003 Annual Report* (Sinopec Corp., 2004a).

Table 6.4   Top Ten Shareholders of Sinopec Corp. as of June 30, 2004

Name of company	Nature of shareholders	Type of shares held	Number of shares held (1,000 shares)	Percentage of total shareholding
China Petroleum and Chemical Corporation (Sinopec Group Company)	State-owned shares	Non-tradable	47,742,561	55.06%
HKSCC (Nominees) Limited[a]	H shares	Tradable	16,676,244	19.23%
China Development Bank	State-owned shares	Non-tradable	8,775,570	10.12%
China Cinda Asset Management Corp.	State-owned shares	Non-tradable	8,720,650	10.06%
China Orient Asset Management Corp.	State-owned shares	Non-tradable	1,296,410	1.50%
Guo Tai Jun An Corp.	State-owned shares	Non-tradable	586,760	0.68%
Qingdao Port Authority	A shares	Tradable	60,000	0.07%
EFUND 50 Securities Investment Fund	A shares	Tradable	51,906	0.06%
Xinghua Securities Investment Fund	A shares	Tradable	48,190	0.06%
Xinghe Securities Investment Fund	A shares	Tradable	46,149	0.05%
CITIC Securities Co., Ltd.	A shares	Tradable	44,485	0.05%

[a] HKSCC (Nominees) Limited held 99.38% of H shares.
Source: Sinopec *Interim Report 2004* (Sinopec Corp., 2004d).

Table 6.5 Top Ten Shareholders of Sinopec Corp. as of December 31, 2007

Name of company	Nature of shareholders	Number of shares held (1,000 shares)	Percentage of total shareholding
China Petroleum and Chemical Corporation (Sinopec Group Company)	State-owned shares	65,758,044	75.84%
HKSCC (Nominees) Limited	H shares	16,699,595	19.26%
Guotai Junan Securities Co., Ltd.	State-owned legal person shares	579,906	0.67%
EFUND 50 Securities Investment Fund	A shares	130,790	0.15%
Shanghai Stock Exchange Tradable Open-end Index Securities Investment Fund	A shares	84,725	0.10%
Harvest Shanghai & Shenzhen 300 Index Securities Investment Fund	A shares	75,918	0.09%
Bosera Thematic Sector Equity Securities Investment Fund	A shares	70,229	0.08%
Bank of Communication Schroders Blue Chip Securities Investment Fund	A shares	50,257	0.06%
China Post Core Growth Securities Investment Fund	A shares	44,000	0.05%
China Life Insurance Company Limited–Dividend–Individual Dividend–005L–FH002 Shanghai	A shares	37,000	0.04%

Source: Sinopec 2007 Annual Report (Sinopec, 2007).

Tables 6.1, 6.2, 6.3, 6.4 and 6.5 show that Sinopec Group Company is the majority shareholder of the company. According to Table 6.1, as of June 2001, Sinopec Group Company held about 56.90% of State-owned shares (which were also non-tradable) in Sinopec Corp., and Tables 6.2, 6.3 and 6.4 show that from December 2002 to June 2004, the total shareholding of Sinopec Group Company remained unchanged at 55.06% (non-tradable, State-owned shares). Apart from Sinopec Group Company, there were other investment companies that only held a small percentage of shares in Sinopec. According to Table 6.5, Sinopec Group's shareholding increased to 75.84%. Given that the Sinopec Group Company is still an SOE, Sinopec Corp. remained a typical product of the economic and enterprise reform in China—a listed company controlled by a dominant state owner of shares.

In the outsider-based model which is reflected in the governance model in listed resources companies in Australia (discussed earlier in this book), one of the major causes of corporate governance problems is the separation of ownership and control. For example, as demonstrated in case studies of BHP Billiton and Rio Tinto, generally, there are no substantial shareholders that hold more than 5% of total shares; this potentially gives rise to an agency problem, which is common in companies with a dispersed ownership structure. In contrast, in the case of Sinopec, the major shareholder usually holds a block of more than 50% of total shares; this suggests that there could exist multi-agency problems, i.e., the minority shareholder's interest could be harmed not only by management, but also by the majority shareholder.

In regard to foreign ownership, Table 6.1 also illustrates that as of June 30, 2001, ExxonMobil, Shell and BP, each held 3.1 billion, 1.9 billion and 1.8 billion shares in Sinopec, which accounted for 3.78%, 2.34% and 2.18% of total shareholdings, respectively. The shareholdings of these three companies together accounted for 8.3% of issued shares and about 40% of issued H shares. The reason that these three companies held a large amount of Sinopec shares was that these companies were promised equity in exchange for a market-based arrangement, namely, their subscribing to shares issued by Sinopec Group Company in exchange for allowing them to establish gas stations in China (Nolan, 2001).

Tables 6.2, 6.3 and 6.4 show that since 2003, ExxonMobil, Shell and BP started to relinquish their shareholdings in Sinopec Corp. BP sold its shares in late 2003, with Shell following suit in early 2004 (Ye, 2004). By mid-2004, both BP and Shell sold their shares (BP plc, 2004; Ye, 2004) and only ExxonMobil was still holding Sinopec shares. According to Table 6.5, none of these companies remained in the list of top ten shareholders in Sinopec as of the report date of Sinopec's 2007 annual report.

Sinopec Corporate Structure and Its Governance Implications

The ownership structure in Sinopec suggests that the corporate structure of Sinopec needs to be studied closely. This structure is illustrated in Figure 6.1.

As demonstrated in Figure 6.1, Sinopec shareholders appoint the board of directors; with a 75% shareholding, the government would appoint most of these directors. The board then appoints the president of Sinopec Corp., and the secretary of the board. Under the leadership of the board, there are three board sub-committees, i.e., an audit committee, a strategic comittee and a compensation committee. Apart from the board of directors, there is also a supervisory board. Sinopec's subsidiaries and sub-branches are also listed in Figure 6.1. Superficially, the only difference between the governance structure of Sinopec and BHP Billiton is that there also exists a supervisory board in Sinopec Corp. However, the fact that there is a dominant State shareholder holding more than 50% of the total shares in Sinopec really casts doubt on the effectiveness of the governance structure in Figure 6.1. This is especially so given the parallel party organization existing alongside the formal organs of the company. The current governance arrangement and its overlap with the previous system led by the committee of the Communist Party was discussed in detail in Chapter 4. On Sinopec Corp's website,[6] the company also lists its subsidiaries which include 16 holding companies. Table 6.6 provides a brief overview of these 16 holding companies.

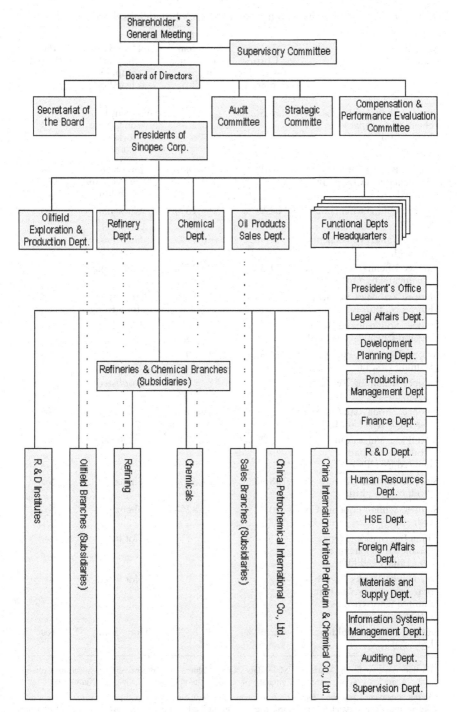

Figure 6.1 Corporate structure of Sinopec Corp. Source: Sinopec Corp. website: http://english.sinopec.com/en-newsevent/en-news/print.html.

Table 6.6 Pyramid Ownership in Sinopec Corp.'s Listed Subsidiaries[a]

(1) Subsidiary name	(2) Sinopec Corp.'s ownership interest	(3) Actual government interest[b]	(4) Stock exchange that the company is listed on	(5) On the top 100 China list 2004 (Yes/no)
Sinopec Shanghai Petro-chemical Company Limited (SPC)	55.56%	30.59%	Shanghai, Hong Kong, New York and London	Yes
Sinopec Beijing Yanhua Petrochemical Company Limited	70%	38.54%	Hong Kong, New York and London	Yes
Sinopec Qilu Petrochemical Co. Ltd	82.05%	45.18%	Shanghai	Yes
Sinopec Yangzi Petrochemical Co., Ltd.	84.98%	46.79%	Shenzhen	Yes
Sinopec Zhenhai Refining & Chemical Co., Ltd.	71.32%	39.27%	Hong Kong	Yes
Sinopec Yizheng Chemical Fibre Co., Ltd.	42%	23.13%	Shanghai and Hong Kong	Yes
Sinopec Shijiazhuang Refin-ing and Chemical Co., Ltd.	79.73%	43.90%	Shenzhen	Yes
Sinopec Shengli Oilfield Daming Co., Ltd.	26.33%	14.50%	Shenzhen	No
Sinopec Maoming Refining & Chemical Co., Ltd.			Not listed	
Sinopec Zhongyuan Oil & Gas High-tech Co., Ltd.	70.85%	39.01%	Shenzhen	No
SINOPEC Wuhan Oil Products Company Limited (WOPC)	46.25%	25.47%	Shenzhen	No
Sinopec Taishan Oil Products Co., Ltd.	38.68%	21.30%	Shenzhen	No
Sinopec Wuhan Phoenix Co., Ltd.	40.72%	22.42%	Shenzhen	No
China International United Petroleum & Chemicals Co., Ltd. (UNIPEC)			Not listed	
Petro-CyberWorks Informa-tion Technology Company Limited (shortened as PCITC)			Not listed	
Sinopec Kantons Holding, Ltd.	72.34%	39.83%	Hong Kong	Yes

[a] The data was complied by Xinting Jia. Major data sources: Column (1) from Sinopec Corp.'s website; Columns (2) and (4) are from various companies' annual reports and Column (3) was calculated by Xinting Jia.

[b] As the State-owned Sinopec Group Company owns 55.06% of Sinopec Corp., by investing in the subsidiaries of Sinopec Corp. through Sinopec Corp., the government has leveraged its control of a group of companies through the so-called pyramid ownership structure. The comparison of real interest is listed in this column.

As is evident in Table 6.6, among those sixteen holding companies, ten are listed on China's domestic A-share market; five are listed on the Hong Kong Stock Exchange and two are listed in New York and on the London Stock Exchanges. In addition, eight of those 16 holding companies were also among the list of the top 100 listed companies in China published by *Fortune* magazine in 2004.

After 2004, Sinopec Beijing Yanhua Petrochemical Company was delisted and merged into Sinopec Corp. after gaining approval at the general and independent shareholders' meeting (Sinopec Corp., 2004e). All the tradable shares were to be bought back by Sinopec Corp. The reason for the share buy-back was suggested by the company as follows: "[Sinopec Corp. and Yanhua]. . . are engaged in the petrochemical business with similar products and competing sales channels" (Sinopec Corp., 2004e). The merger was intended not only to eliminate intra-group competition (Sinopec Corp., 2004e), it also alleviated the governance problems of Sinopec Corp. caused by the complicated pyramid structure of the company.

Related Party Transactions and Corporate Governance

According to Zhang (2004), related party transactions are an inherent problem in China, due largely to the way that listed companies developed in China. In Sinopec's case, as shown in Table 6.5, all these listed companies were part of the Sinopec Group before they were listed on the stock market; therefore, there existed numerous related party transactions (both legitimate and illegitimate) among those companies before as well as after those companies were listed. The share buy-back of Sinopec Beijing Yanhua by Sinopec Corp. has helped internalize some of these related party transactions and make these of less concern to the public.

The Composition of the Board at Sinopec

The composition of the board in Sinopec Corp. is quite different from the boards of BHP Billiton and Rio Tinto. Because of the existence of a dominant state shareholder and the controlling relationship between the party and the government, board members in Sinopec were appointed by the government and the party. Examination of board members' biographies (available on Sinopec's website and in its annual reports) clearly illustrate the influence of the party and the government over the appointment of board members.

In 2005, the board of directors of Sinopec comprised 13 members; all of these directors were elected at the general shareholders' meeting in 2003 and the term of their appointment was to be three years (i.e., until 2006). Among those 13 directors, four were independent directors.

As described on Sinopec's website (Sinopec Corp., 2004b), directors other than independent directors were chosen according to the following rule:

> Candidates for non-independent directors are nominated by Sinopec's board of directors, the supervisory committee, or shareholders who hold 5% *or more* of the Company's voting shares. (Sinopec Corp., 2004b: 1)

Shareholders that held 5% or more shares as stated in 2007 are listed in Table 6.7.

As shown in Table 6.7, the majority shareholder held 75.84% of total shares in Sinopec; these shares will gradually become tradable. In terms of the shares held by HKSCC, because the HKSCC was a nominee company, the 19.26% of shares under the name of HKSCC only indicated that those shares were registered under HKSCC (Nominees) Limited. There was no clear indication as to whether any shareholder registered with HKSCC (Nominees) Limited actually held 5% or more of the total shares in Sinopec Corp. Since Sinopec Group Company controlled more than 75% of total shares of Sinopec Corp., it had the ultimate control right of electing non-independent directors in Sinopec Corp.

The composition of the board showed that the chairman of the board was also the president of the Sinopec Group. There was another director who was the vice-president of the Sinopec Group. Four directors held various senior management roles ranging from president and vice-president to chief financial officer of Sinopec Corp. The chairman of the board of Sinopec Shengli Oil Field (a subsidiary of Sinopec Corp.) was elected as one of the employee representatives. Independent directors of the company were elected according to the following rule: ". . . shareholders who individually or jointly own 1% or more of the Company's voting shares can nominate candidates for independent directors" (Sinopec Corp., 2004b: 1).

Table 6.7   Shareholders of Sinopec Holding More Than 5% of Shares in 2007

Name of company	Nature of shareholders	Number of shares held (1,000 shares)	Percentage of total shareholding
China Petrochemical Corporation (Sinopec Group Company)	State-owned shares	65,758,044	75.84%
HKSCC (Nominees) Limited	H shares	16,699,595	19.26%

Source: *2007 Sinopec Annual Report* (Sinopec, 2007).

According to Sinopec, the following criteria were also used to evaluate the independence of a director (Sinopec Corp., 2004b: 1); directors would be classified as independent by Sinopec so long as they are not:

1. Employed, or related to a family member employed by Sinopec or its subsidiaries
2. Direct or indirect holders of 1% or more of Sinopec's issued shares, or, with their family members, are not among the top ten shareholders
3. Employed by a shareholder company which directly or indirectly holds 5% or more of the company's issued shares, or, along with immediate family members, among the top five shareholders
4. Members of nos. 1 to 3 for the past one year
5. Providing financial or legal advice to the company or its subsidiaries
6. Already a director of five listed companies
7. Other persons as determined by the securities regulatory authority of the State Council as deemed incapable of serving as an independent director

All four independent directors of Sinopec Corp. have also worked for the government. Three of the four directors were members of the Standing Committee of the Chinese People's Political Consultative Committee and one was a member of the Standing Committee of the National People's Congress.

In general, the major shareholder was well represented on the board, and there are no minority representatives on the board. Superficially, board composition is an indication of the company's new governance structure; however, a close look at the board's composition suggests that the old management team of the state-owned enterprise remains in place; this might be referred to as "filling a new bottle with old wine." Some people argue that this has occurred because China has taken a gradualist approach in its economic and enterprise reform effort.

Similar to arrangements found in Australia, listed companies in China are required by the China Securities Regulatory Commission (CSRC) to set up specialized committees of their boards. In Sinopec Corp., the following subcommittees have been set up within the board: (i) the Strategic Planning Committee, (ii) the Audit Committee and (iii) the Remuneration and Evaluation Committee.

Composition of the Supervisory Board at Sinopec

Chinese Company Law requires that companies appoint a supervisory board. The supervisory board of Sinopec has nine members; only one of these members is independent. Among the remaining eight members, the chairman and vice-chairman of the supervisory board and two other supervisors also hold senior management positions with the Sinopec Group, while four other supervisors were named employee representatives; they all hold senior management positions and party secretary positions with subsidiaries or related entities of Sinopec. This composition casts doubt on whether they will really represent employees' interests. Despite this, there has been some improvement since its previous composition in 2004. Back then, there were 12 members appointed to the supervisory board and among them, eight members were shareholder representatives. Among these eight members, six held senior management positions within the Sinopec Group and two were independent supervisory board members. Among the four employee representatives, two were presidents of the unions of Sinopec Group's subsidiaries, one supervisory board member was the party leader of one of Sinopec Group's subsidiaries and one member was the president of one of Sinopec Group's subsidiaries. The chairman of the supervisory board was also the assistant to the president of the Sinopec Group (who was the chairman of the board of Sinopec Corp.). In terms of the employee representatives on the board, two were presidents of the union in the Sinopec Group's subsidiaries. In China, the president of the union is normally a member of the Communist Party and is also appointed by the government. So, in Sinopec's case, the supervisory board more or less represents the interests of government; this stands in stark contrast to the role of the union on the supervisory boards in Germany, where they more clearly do represent the interests of workers.

Stakeholders and Corporate Governance at Sinopec

Sinopec's website and annual reports make no specific mention of those who are the stakeholders of the company and whether their interests are considered in the governance of the company. However, for historical reasons, employees were treated as one of the more important stakeholders in SOEs in China (Jia, 2004). Therefore, the following discussion of the role of stakeholders in corporate governance is focused on the role of employees in corporate governance. Because employee representatives on the supervisory board are appointed by the government, it is unlikely that those employee representatives will effectively stand for the interests of employees in cases of a conflicts of interest between the government and company employees.

In terms of whether employee interests have been considered in making corporate decisions, in 2005 the government required that Sinopec transfer 5–10% of its net profits to the statutory welfare fund for the construction of dormitories, canteens and other staff welfare facilities before it made a dividend distribution (Sinopec, 2005: 80). This indicated that employee welfare was seen as a very important issue. Sinopec was also required to make contributions (normally ranging from 17% to 30% of the salaries, bonuses and certain allowances of its staff) to defined retirement plans organized by municipal and provincial governments (Sinopec, 2005: 99). This stood in contrast to the practice that existed prior to the reforms that led to the formation of the company; at that time, an entity that had the form of an SOE was required to pay pensions directly to its retirees. This change in practice indicates that the company is gradually relieving itself of some of its social responsibilities to employees and to society. Overall, this practice is consistent with the gradualist approach adopted by the government in its economic and enterprise reform effort in China.

Summary

Sinopec provides a good example of how a leading enterprise has evolved in the economic and enterprise reform process in China. It also demonstrates that government, as a dominant shareholder, still plays a very important role in shaping company policies (corporate governance policies in this analysis) and that their implementation in former SOEs that have been transformed into listed companies. Overall, the case of Sinopec demonstrates that the PRC government plays a very important role in promoting and implementing corporate governance in listed companies, even though the current stage of implementation of such rules only focuses on formality rather than substance. In general, the gradualist approach adopted by the government in promoting corporate governance is consistent with the overall strategies of economic and enterprise reform in China.

THE CASE OF BAOSHAN IRON & STEEL CO., LTD.

To further compare and contrast the cases of industry leaders discussed in Chapter 5, a company from the metals industry—Baoshan Iron & Steel Co., Ltd.—was chosen for our second Chinese case study. Baoshan Iron & Steel Co., Ltd. (hereinafter referred to as "Baoshan Iron & Steel") originated from Baosteel Group Corporation (hereinafter referred to as 'Baosteel Group'). Baosteel Group is one of the oldest iron and steel companies in China. Like most other big iron and steel companies in China, the Baosteel Group was under the direct control of the Ministry of Metallurgy prior to 1998.

In 1998, a reform plan by the State Council reduced the number of ministries from forty to twenty-nine (Chen, 1998), with the Ministry of Metallurgy being downgraded to a bureau under the State Economic and Trade Commission (SETC) (Chen, 1998). Baoshan Iron & Steel was formed within the Baosteel Group in February 2000 and was listed on the Shanghai Stock Exchange in December in the same year (Baoshan Iron & Steel Co., Ltd., 2005c). In 2001, when SASAC was formed to manage state interests in major listed companies in China, the control of Baosteel Group was transferred to SASAC. Now the Baosteel Group is one of the 169 companies that are under the direct control of SASAC. The Baosteel Group is China's largest steel maker (Yahoo, 2006) and has 12 subsidiaries as illustrated in Figure 6.2.

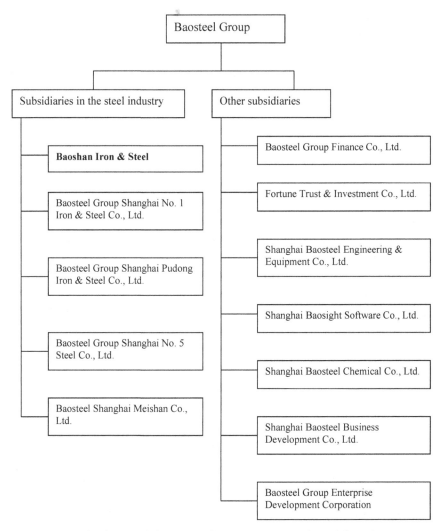

Figure 6.2   Subsidiaries of the Baosteel Group. Source: adapted from http://www.baosteel.com.

As illustrated in Figure 6.2, Baoshan Iron & Steel is one of 12 subsidiaries of the Baosteel Group. Among these 12 subsidiaries, five operate in the steel industry and seven operate in other industries. Baoshan Iron & Steel is also a typical product of China's unique economic and enterprise reforms, as it was formed by grouping the best-performing assets of the Baosteel Group in a new listed corporate entity; this was to ensure the successful listing of Baoshan Iron & Steel on the stock exchange. This practice has been quite common in SOEs that have been transformed into listed companies, as it helps to minimize the downside risk associated with the overall economic and enterprise reform process in China.

Corporate Structure of Baoshan Iron & Steel

The corporate structure of Baoshan Iron & Steel is illustrated in Figure 6.3. The general structure of the company is very similar to the structure of Sinopec in that the shareholders' assembly appoints the board of directors, which then appoints the president of the company. Apart from the board of directors, there is also a supervisory board in Baoshan Iron & Steel.

As illustrated in Figure 6.3, apart from the governance structure of Baoshan Iron & Steel, the functional departments and subsidiaries of the company are also set out.

To further understand the corporate structure of Baoshan Iron & Steel and its corporate governance, the following themes will be explored in the following sections: the ownership structure of the company and the future outlook of the company following the split share structure reforms; issues related to related party transactions; the composition of the board and the company's supervisory board and its governance implications; and the role of stakeholders, especially of employees, in corporate governance.

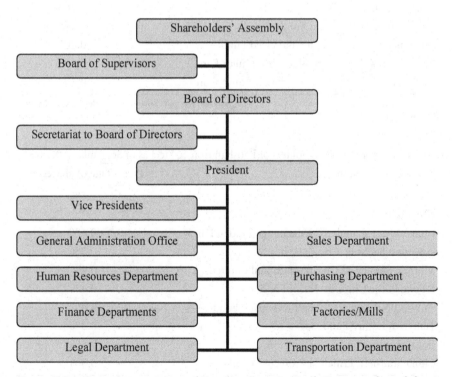

Figure 6.3 Corporate structure of Baoshan Iron & Steel. Source: adapted from http://www.baosteel.com/.

The Ownership Structure of Baoshan Iron & Steel and Its Implications for Corporate Governance

Baoshan Iron & Steel is a typical listed company that has emerged from a previously state-owned enterprise. As illustrated in Tables 6.8, 6.9, 6.10, 6.11 and 6.12, the dominant shareholder was the Baosteel Group—an SOE. The top ten shareholders are also listed in Tables 6.8, 6.9, 6.10, 6.11 and 6.12.[7]

Table 6.8 Top Ten Shareholders of Baoshan Iron & Steel as of 2007

Name of the shareholder	Percentage of shares held
Baosteel Group	73.97%
Harvest Stable Open Fund	0.61%
China Life Insurance Company Limited—Dividend–Individual Dividend—FH002 Shanghai	0.51%
China Post & Capital Core Enhanced Equity Fund	0.47%
China Life Insurance Company Limited—Traditional–General Insurance Product	0.47%
E Funds Blue Chip 50 Index Fund	0.46%
Industrial Trend Invested Fund	0.41%
E Funds Growth and Value Balanced Fund	0.40%
Invesco Great Wall Core Blue Chip Equity Fund	0.39%
China Post & Capital Core Growth Equity Fund	0.36%

Source: *Baoshan Iron & Steel Co. Third-Quarter Report 2007*, available at http://www.baosteel.com/.

Table 6.9 Top Ten Shareholders of Baoshan Iron & Steel as of September 30, 2005

Name of the shareholder	Percentage of shares held
Baosteel Group	75.5%
UBS Limited	0.7%
China AMC Shanghai 50 Exchange Traded Fund	0.6%
Goldman Sachs & Co.	0.5%
Morgan Stanley & Co. International Limited	0.4%
E Funds Blue Chips 50 Index Fund	0.4%
SYWG BNP Paribas Shengli Enhanced Fund	0.4%
Tianyuan Equity Fund	0.3%
Jingfu Equity Fund	0.3%
China Southern Principal Protected Fund	0.3%

Source: *Baoshan Iron & Steel Co. Third-Quarter Report 2005*, available at http://www.baosteel.com/.

Table 6.10   Top Ten Shareholders of Baoshan Iron & Steel as of June 30, 2005

Name of the shareholder	Percentage of shares held
Baosteel Group	77.86%
China AMC Shanghai 50 Exchange Traded Fund	0.81%
Fortis Haitong Growth & Income Fund	0.54%
UBS Limited	0.44%
E Funds Blue Chips 50 Index Fund	0.43%
Morgan Stanley & Co. International Limited	0.33%
Anshun Equity Fund	0.31%
Bosera Enhanced Equity Fund	0.30%
Fenghe Value Fund	0.29%
CITIC Classical Allocation Fund	0.29%
SYWG BNP Paribas Enhanced Fund	0.26%

Source: *Baoshan Iron & Steel Interim Report 2005*, available at http://www.baosteel.com/.

Table 6.11   Top Ten Shareholders of Baoshan Iron & Steel as of December 31, 2004

Name of the shareholder	Percentage of shares held
Baosteel Group	85%
E Funds Blue Chip 50 Index Fund	0.56%
SYWG BNP Paribas Enhanced Fund	0.32%
UBS Limited	0.30%
Anshun Equity Fund	0.29%
Fenghe Value Fund	0.26%
Galaxy Yintai Dividend Fund	0.25%
Bosera Enhanced Equity Fund	0.25%
Fortis Haitong Income Fund	0.25%
Hua'an Fund Management	0.24%
Deutsche Bank	0.24%

Source: *Baoshan Iron & Steel Co., Ltd. Annual Report 2004*, available at http://www.baosteel.com/.

Table 6.12   Top Ten Shareholders of Baoshan Iron & Steel as of December 31, 2003

Name of the shareholder	Percentage of shares held
Baosteel Group	85%
UBS Limited	0.70%
Hua'an Innovation Fund	0.31%
Kerui Fund	0.27%
Tongsheng Fund	0.26
Tongyi Fund	0.24%
Yinfeng Fund	0.20%
Tianyuan Fund	0.18%
Bosera Value & Growth Fund	0.13%
E Funds Strategic Growth Fund	0.13%
Jintai Fund	0.12%

Source: *Baoshan Iron & Steel Co., Ltd. Annual Report 2003*, available at http://www.baosteel.com/.

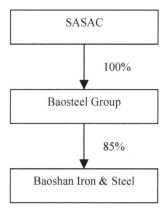

Figure 6.4 The relationship of SASAC, Baosteel Group and Baoshan Iron & Steel. Source: translated by Xinting Jia from *Annual Report 2004* of Baoshan Iron and Steel, which is available at http://www.baosteel.com/.

As shown in Tables 6.8, 6.9, 6.10, 6.11 and 6.12, although the percentage of shares held by the Baosteel Group fell from 85% in 2003 to 73.97% in 2007, the state-owned shares remained in the dominant position. In fact, the drop in the percentage of state shares from 85% to 73.97% resulted mainly from the split share ownership structure reforms. In order to allow non-tradable shares (held by the dominant shareholder) to be tradable, the dominant shareholder needed to allocate a certain amount of its non-tradable shares to minority shareholders.

In terms of the ownership structure of Baoshan Iron & Steel, the state interest in the company was ultimately controlled by SASAC; this is illustrated in Figure 6.4.

Corporate governance in Baoshan Iron & Steel needs to be studied carefully for two reasons: first, as an enterprise controlled directly by SASAC, Baoshan Iron & Steel was part of the second round of companies chosen to experiment with the split share ownership structure reforms. Until 2007, about 6% of the shares held by Baosteel Group had already became tradable. Second, as illustrated in Tables 6.8, 6.9, 6.10, 6.11 and 6.12, Qualified Foreign Institutional Investors (QFIIs) are also among the top ten shareholders of Baosteel; therefore, this could also help us explore the QFIIs' role in corporate governance.

The Split Share Ownership Structure Reform in Baoshan Iron & Steel

The PRC government's recent split share ownership structure reform has been another landmark in China's economic and enterprise reforms. It aims to resolve the split share ownership structure that has existed in

Table 6.13   The Progress of the Split Share Ownership Structure Reform in Baoshan Iron & Steel

Date	Event
June 20, 2005	Public notice regarding the trial of reforming the split share ownership structure plan in Baoshan Iron & Steel was issued.
June 27, 2005	The reform plan was submitted for discussion to the first special shareholders' meeting in 2005.
August 12, 2005	The split share ownership structure reform plan was approved by the first special shareholders' meeting (through both voting at the meeting and voting via the Internet).

Source: translated by Xinting Jia from *Baoshan Iron and Steel 2005 Interim Report*; the report is available at http://www.baosteel.com/.

most listed companies in China. Split share ownership refers to the fact that in a listed company, the majority of the shares were non-tradable and were held by an SOE; the remaining shares were tradable and were held by minority shareholders. An overview of the split share ownership structure reforms in China was provided in Chapter 1. This reform was first initiated in May 2005. Baoshan Iron & Steel was among the 42 firms to first experiment with the reform in June 2005 (People's Daily Online, 2005b). The detailed reform plan for Baoshan Iron & Steel was released and approved by shareholders on August 12, 2005. Initial progress in the split share ownership structure reforms can be seen in Table 6.13.

By the end of 2007, almost all listed companies in China have initiated their split share ownership reforms. Here, we discuss how the reform was implemented at a firm level using Baosteel as an example. As the dominant shareholder, Baosteel Group has made formal commitments to implement its split share ownership structure reforms; as illustrated in its *Interim Report 2005* (Baoshan Iron & Steel Co., Ltd., 2005a: 19–20).[8] The company expressed this goal as follows:

1. Baosteel Group shall strictly follow the split share ownership structure reform plan as approved by the shareholder's meeting. The amount of non-tradable shares that need to be allocated to tradable shareholders will be formally transferred to and be under the custody of the Shanghai Branch of the China Securities Depository and Clearing Corporation Limited to ensure Baosteel Group's fulfilment of this commitment.
2. Baosteel Group is also committed to the following: within the first two months of the approval of the split share ownership structure reform plan, if the share price of Baoshan Iron & Steel drops below RMB ¥ 4.53 per share, the Baosteel Group shall increase its shareholding by purchasing from the market; the total spending shall be no

more than RMB ¥ 2 billion. This commitment will be fulfilled within a two months period unless the share price is no less than RMB ¥ 4.53 per share or the amount of RMB¥ 2 billion is depleted. Baosteel shall strictly follow the rules of information disclosure and shall not sell the increased shares within six months of executing such share increase plan.

3. Baosteel shall strictly follow the requirement in the Circular on Issues relating to the Pilot Reform of Listed Companies' Split Share Structure (*guanyu shangshi gongsi guquan fenzhi gaige shidian youguan wenti de tongzhi*) in that in the first 12 months after the shares held by Baosteel Group become tradable, Baosteel shall not trade or transfer its shares; in the first 24 months after the shares held by Baosteel become tradable, Baosteel shall not trade its shares; in the next 12 months after the first initial 24 months that the shares held by Baosteel Group become tradable, the total shares sold in the stock exchange shall not be more than 5% of the total shares issued by Baoshan Iron & Steel, with a price of no less than RMB ¥ 5.63 per share. Within the three years that the shares held by the Baosteel Group become tradable, the number of shares held by the Baosteel Group shall not be less than 67% of the total shares issued by Baoshan Iron & Steel. However, the shares increased according to item 2 above shall not be subject to the restrictions stipulated in this item.

4. To further promote the split share structure reform, Baosteel Group also commits that within six months after the initial two months period as stipulated in item 2, if the share price of Baoshan Iron & Steel drops below RMB ¥ 4.53, Baosteel Group shall further invest another RMB ¥ 2 billion plus the remaining funds (if any) from the initial RMB ¥ 2 billion committed, to purchase the shares of Baoshan Iron & Steel on the stock exchange. Baosteel Group shall not sell its shares within the 6 months of its share increase.

This detailed plan further illustrates that the focus of the split share ownership structure reforms was not to dilute state ownership but rather to explore an avenue for converting the state's non-tradable shares into tradable shares, thereby ensuring that shares held by the dominant shareholders would have the same rights and responsibilities as those of holders of tradable shares. The performance of the dominant shareholder can also be gauged by the fluctuation of the share price in the market.

In Baoshan Iron & Steel's *Third-Quarter Report 2005* (Baoshan Iron & Steel Co., Ltd., 2005b), the company also provided an update on how the above commitments were fulfilled. In terms of item 2, the Baosteel Group holding in Baoshan Iron & Steel had increased by a total of 446,565,849 shares from August 25, 2005 to September 21, 2005 and it had used up all of the RMB ¥ 2 billion that it had promised. The Baosteel Group also started to purchase more shares from the stock market using the second lot of RMB ¥ 2 billion it promised, as described in item 4.

The split share ownership structure reforms in Baoshan Iron & Steel illustrate that the major aim of these reforms was not to flood the market with a sudden increase in the number of tradable shares but to give the major shareholder more flexibility once the company's shares becomes tradable. It will also allow the government to adjust its shareholdings in various industries so as to suit its overall policies. Furthermore, it could also give the government more power in disciplining the controllers of listed companies by using the change in share price as a barometer.

QFIIs' Role in Corporate Governance

As illustrated in Tables 6.9, 6.10, 6.11 and 6.12, in the period from 2003 to 2005, some of the Qualified Foreign Institutional Investors (QFIIs), such as UBS Limited, Goldman Sachs & Co., Morgan Stanley & Co. International Limited and Deutsche Bank have been purchasing shares in Baoshan Iron & Steel. However, the percentage of shares owned by those QFIIs was largely immaterial (normally less than 1% of the total shares in the company); also the ownership of these shares was very unstable over the two year period, indicating frequent trading of shares by QFIIs rather than their holding of these shares over the long term.

Interviews with company secretaries and other controllers of listed companies in China suggest that the QFII scheme may eventually play a role in improving corporate governance in China's listed companies. However, the data suggests that the present role of QFIIs in improving corporate governance in Baoshan Iron & Steel is rather limited (as they generally only hold small amounts of shares and do so for relatively short periods of time).

Related Party Transactions and Corporate Governance at Baosteel

Related party transactions are clearly disclosed in Baoshan Iron & Steel's annual reports as well as in its interim reports. As disclosed in its 2003 and 2004 annual reports, about 66.79% and 72% of sales of the company's products in 2003 and 2004, respectively involved Baoshan International and its subsidiaries. Baoshan Iron & Steel also disclosed in detail related party transactions in the areas of purchasing raw materials, assets and share ownership transfers, etc. Most of the related parties of Baoshan Iron & Steel were subsidiaries of the Baosteel Group; this demonstrates that despite the listing of Baoshan Iron & Steel, it still operates as if it was a unit of the Baosteel Group. As also discussed in the case of Sinopec, related party transactions are an inherent problem in most listed companies in China. However, the existence of related party transactions does not necessarily mean that they are inappropriate. As long as related party transactions are conducted at arms length or on a commercial basis, they will not jeopardize the integrity of the company's corporate governance. The detailed disclosure of related party transactions in its annual reports also suggests transparency in Baosteel's disclosures.

Composition of the Board of Baosteel

The composition of the board, supervisory board and senior management team of Baoshan Iron & Steel is reported on its website. Apart from four executive directors, all three of the other non-executive directors are senior executives of the Baosteel Group. This once again illustrates the dominant position of the majority shareholder in appointing directors. Two board sub-committees have also been established; they are: (i) the remuneration and performance evaluation committee; and (ii) the audit committee. Both committees are chaired by independent directors and are also mainly composed of independent directors.

Composition of the Supervisory Board of Baosteel

The members of the supervisory board and their work history and educational background are also listed on the company's website. Among the nine supervisors of the company, there are three executive supervisors (who are also described as employee representatives by the company), three non-executive supervisors (who are all from the Baosteel Group) and three independent supervisors.

As stated in Baoshan Iron & Steel's *Annual Report 2004*, the major function of the supervisory board is to monitor the functions of the board, monitor the financial affairs of the company as well as to monitor the key strategies of the company. As already discussed in Chapter 4, the fact that the members of the supervisory board were appointed by the company's major shareholder casts doubt on its real functionality. This has been discussed in detail in Chapter 4 based on aggregated interview data with controllers of listed resources companies in China.

Stakeholders and Corporate Governance in Baosteel

The stakeholder's role in corporate governance is focused on the role of employees in corporate governance. As discussed in Chapter 4 as well as in regard to Sinopec, direct participation of employees in corporate governance is very rare in China; this is because trade unions are under the control of the government. However, in most cases, employees' interests have been considered in corporate governance for historical reasons. Under the planned economy, SOEs were required to provide various services such as free housing, medical care and a general pension to its employees. Because of the gradualist approach adopted by China in its economic reforms, those practices will only gradually fade as a more reliable social security system is established in China (Jia, 2004).

The gradualist approach of relieving itself of its social responsibility role to its employees was clearly illustrated in Baoshan Iron and Steel. As stated in the company's 2003 annual report, the company was still financially supporting 178 semi-retired employees (Baoshan Iron & Steel Co., Ltd., 2003). However, in the following year's report, it stated that the company was no longer providing financial support directly to its retirees (Baoshan Iron & Steel Co., Ltd., 2004). The company also allocated 10% of its net profits in 2003 and 2004 to a special fund, known as the Statutory Public Welfare Fund, which provided for employee-welfare-related matters.

CONCLUSION

The case study of Baoshan Iron & Steel demonstrates that government involvement in corporate governance in listed resources companies in China is still extensive. However, the implementation of the split share ownership structure reforms is likely to give the government more flexibility so as to allow it to rely on market mechanisms rather than merely on its administrative measures to govern listed companies.

Compared with companies such as BHP Billiton, Rio Tinto, Shell and Chevron, the two Chinese companies discussed in this chapter demonstrate the unique characteristics of corporate governance in China: these include an ownership structure with the government being the majority shareholder, the existence of a supervisory board as well as a management board, and the dominance of executive directors on both boards. Major stakeholder roles in relation to corporate governance (such as those of employees) were also explored in this chapter and found to be of limited effect in China's resources companies. Other wider stakeholder interests, such as those relating to the environment, will be examined in Chapter 7.

7 Governing Resources Companies and Corporate Social Responsibility
Can China Do Better?

INTRODUCTION

Should companies fulfill their social responsibilities and protect stakeholder interests while pursuing profit-seeking objectives? While debate continues on the legitimacy of corporate social responsibility (CSR) (Bakan, 2004), there is an emerging consensus among many leading companies that stakeholder interests should be protected at least to a certain extent so as to avoid bad publicity. This is especially true for resources companies as most are large multinational companies and have their reputation (brand value) at risk. In addition, resources companies operate in a high-risk industry associated with the challenges of maintaining the health and safety of their workers, and protecting communities and the environment.

Mirroring the fast growth that has occurred in the Chinese economy, resources companies in China have also grown rapidly and have gained more worldwide publicity in recent years. As these Chinese companies become more active globally, they have also started to work more closely with their Western counterparts. However, there is some urgency about increasing our understanding not only of their general governance practices (as we discussed in the previous chapters) but also of how they deal with CSR and stakeholder protection in their business practices. These issues are of vital importance to the proper management and the further development of these resources companies.

This chapter looks at the CSR practices in major Chinese listed companies with an emphasis on those in the resources sector. Before we look at their CSR practices, the definition of CSR and its historical development needs first to be explored.

CSR DEFINITION AND DEBATE

In one of the first attempts to define CSR, Beesley and Evans argued that CSR involves a " . . . relative shift from government to companies as the source of social improvement and the means to promote specific items of social welfare" (Beesley and Evans, 1978: 13).

In a broader sense, CSR involves four layers of responsibility: economic, legal, ethical and philanthropic. Economic responsibilities refer to the responsibilities of a corporation to "produce goods and services that society wants and to sell them at fair prices" (Carroll and Buchholtz, 2003: 36); legal responsibilities mean that corporations should at least obey the letter of the law—what some refer to as the "codified ethics" (Carroll and Buchholtz, 2003: 36).

Ethical responsibilities, as the term suggests, "embody the full scope of norms, standards, and expectations that reflect a belief of what consumers, employees, shareholders, and the community regard as fair, just and in keeping with the respect for or protection of stakeholders' moral rights" (Carroll and Buchholtz, 2003: 37); and, finally, philanthropic responsibilities might include activities such as "corporate giving, product and service donations, volunteerism" (Carroll and Buchholtz, 2003: 38). This reflects a wider sense of community obligation. According to Standards Australia, CSR simply refers to "a mechanism for entities to voluntarily integrate social and environmental concerns into their operations and their interaction with their stakeholders, which are over and above the entity's legal responsibilities." (Standards Australia, 2003: 4).

Embedded in the CSR approach is the view that stakeholder interests rather than only shareholder interests are considered in managing a corporation. While the wider public awareness of CSR has been somewhat recent, the debate over "promoting stakeholder interests" versus "maximising shareholder value" began as early as 1932 (Berle and Means, 1932) and has continued since the appearance of the word stakeholder in corporate governance debates in 1963 (Alkhafaji, 1989).

On the one hand, mainstream economists argue that promoting stakeholder interests is a total deviation from what corporations should be doing; it violates the principle of respecting property rights and fails to see that managers selected by shareholders are simply agents and should therefore serve the interests of their principal by maximizing profit and hence shareholder wealth (Berle, 1932; Friedman, 1962, 1970).

On the other hand, those who promote stakeholder interests (and hence CSR) argue that: "(1) industrial society faces serious human and social problems brought on by large corporations, and (2) managers must conduct the affairs of the corporation in ways to solve or at least ameliorate these problems" (Carroll and Buchholtz, 2003: 43); in addition, it is argued by some that it is in the long-term interests of businesses to be socially responsible (Dodd, 1932; Carroll and Buchholtz, 2003). Nowadays, the core of the debate is not whether a corporation has social responsibility but rather the debate revolves around how CSR should be defined and how it should be applied.

Along with this debate and the search for suitable definitions of CSR, the meaning of CSR has also changed across time, as illustrated in Table 7.1:

According to Table 7.1, CSR has gradually moved away from being seen as 'ethical' and a commitment to society to being seen as a means of retaining competitiveness and properly managing risk; some have also added that CSR will at the same time also enhance company financial performance (Hawkins, 2006; Hancock, 2005).

In recent years, corporations have realized that to be successful in an increasingly competitive global environment, they have to take a holistic approach to CSR that will not only ensure a return to shareholders, wages to employees and products and services to consumers, but will also help companies to respond proactively to environmental and social issues in a complex global landscape (OECD, 2001: 13).

There are also some global standards promoting CSR; these include the *The OECD Guidelines for Multinational Enterprises*, the *Global Sullivan Principles of Corporate Social Responsibility*, and the *United Nations*

Table 7.1 The Meaning of CSR as Conveyed in the *Financial Times*, 1999–2003

Rhetorical strategy	Logic of argumentation	Typical words	Narrative time
Citing themes associated with CSR	Defines what CSR is about	CSR is a commitment to social and environmental issues; the corporation is a transnational entity and CSR can be practiced at different geographical levels	Present
Describing problems that can occur if CSR is neglected	Bad ethics equals bad businesses	Unethical Crises	The 'old' way of doing business (history)
	Not paying attention to CSR can have unanticipated consequences, i.e., scandals such as Enron	Scandal	
Presenting CSR as a solution	CSR as a success story	Profit	The 'new' way of doing business (present and future)
	Good ethics equals good business	Competitiveness	
		Innovative	
		Risk management	

Source: (Buhr and Grafström, 2007: 23, 28).

Norms on the Responsiblities of Transnational Corporations and Other Business Enterprises with Regard to Human Rights (Mullerat, 2005). A number of regional initiatives also promote CSR, these include the European Iniatives developed by the European Parliament and by the European Commission (Lux et al., 2005). These 'soft law' instruments are of vital importance to promoting best practice in CSR in multinational companies given that these companies operate globally in countries with vastly different social, legal and economic environments, and given the challenges that arise in the regulation of these companies through strictly legal methods (Zerk, 2006; Medjad, 2006; Wilson, 1998).

KEY LEGISLATIVE AND QUASI-LEGISLATIVE DRIVERS OF CSR

Mainstream economists have long believed that pollution and environmental degradation are negative economic externalities of free market economies and that it is the government's responsibility to issue proper regulations to force companies to comply with proper environmental standards (Friedman, 1970). For example, governments can pursue a variety of regulatory options, such as setting up sub-national and sectoral goals and targets, the passage of national environmental laws and standards and the issuance of industry-led 'new regulation' or quasi-standards (Asian Development Bank, 2005: 7).

In each country, apart from the pressure to comply with domestic legislation, other global best practices are to be found that seek to encourage companies to be more socially responsible. These standards include the 1999 United Nations Global Compact, which seeks to encourage companies to report their performance on social and environmental dimensions (The United Nations, 2007) and the Global Reporting Initiative (GRI) which provides a framework for companies to report on their environmental and social performance in association with their financial performance (Global Reporting Initiative, 2008). Another initiative is the Equator Principles (issued by the International Finance Corporation [IFC] of the World Bank), which are a benchmark for the financial industry to manage social and environmental issues in project financing (Equator Principles, 2008). In addition, research shows that giving financial services institutions (such as banks, pension funds and insurance companies) environmental reporting obligations will facilitate investments towards better environmental management across the whole economy (Richardson, 2002).

The 2005 Principles for Responsible Investment (PRI), developed by the United Nations Environment Programme (UNEP), have provided another basis for institutional monitoring of companies in terms of their CSR behaviour. By following these Principles, asset owners and investment managers are required to assess their investments by taking into consideration environmental, social and governance (ESG) criteria, together with the company's financial performance. This will further encourage companies to take up best practices in regard to CSR.

Despite the emergence of regional regulations and global sustainable development initiatives, compliance with these standards is not compulsory and there is variable consistency in compliance. This is especially true in emerging markets, where vast differences have existed in the legal, social and economic environment in each country. In emerging markets in Asia, formal legal rules have had limited impact (Asian Development Bank, 2005).

The Case of China

Turning to China, as we seen from previous chapters, governmental administrative measures remain dominant in governing listed companies. Recently, the Chinese government State-owned Assets Supervision and Administration Commission (SASAC) also issued an official document advising state-owned enterprises (SOEs) on how to fulfil their social responsibility; this was a very symbolic move as it indicated that CSR issues were likely to become a major focus for SASAC in the future (Ho, 2008).

Furthermore, leading resources companies in China are already at the forefront of practicing good CSR. For example, as reported by the Social Investment Research Analyst Network (SIRAN), Sinopec has already made considerable disclosure of its social and environmental practices following the GRI principles (SIRAN, 2008). Sinopec has also achieved a satisfactory result in regard to its compliance with the requirements of the Global Compact (United Nations, 2005: 13). The fact that the Chinese government is its major shareholder also signals that the government supports Sinopec's adoption of good practices in regard to CSR.

MAJOR ISSUES RELATED TO CSR

CSR issues can be categorized into two major types, enviromentally related issues and social issues or concerns. Social concerns can also be sub-categorized into employee-related issues and community-related issues. How companies deal with their environmental and social practice will have an enormous impact on a company's CSR practices. Furthermore, globalization is likely to be a major influence in the development of CSR worldwide (OECD, 2001).

Environmental Issues and the Debate on
Climate Change—China's Case

In the early stages of industrialization in most developed countries, economic prosperity was often gained at a heavy cost to the environment.

China's rapid economic development in the past 30 years has also caused enormous damage to the environment across the country (Smil, 1993). The full scale of the environmental damage that has been caused in various parts of China is almost beyond comprehension (Economy, 2004). In a report issued by the OECD in October 2007, the cost of environmental pollution was assessed and it was found that water scarcity (caused by pollution) alone would cost 147 billion Yuan a year (OECD, 2007: xv).

Environmental issues are said to be of the foremost concern to the Chinese government. In its latest White Paper on Energy Conditions and Policies (Information Office of the State Council of the People's Republic of China, 2007: 4), it is stated that "[the Chinese government] has made it a fundamental policy to strengthen environmental protection" and that China is committed to being "a responsible developing country" in terms of environmental protection and the prevention of global climate change (Information Office of the State Council of the People's Republic of China, 2007: 15).

Compared with companies in other sectors, resources companies remain in a high-risk category in terms of social and environmental risk (Hackett, 1998). This is because environmental and social issues are mainly associated with extractive industries and tend to attract the attention of both the general public and of other groups, such as human rights groups and nongovernmental organizations (NGOs) (Yakovleva, 2005). For that reason, the reputational risk associated with negative publicity has also increased for these types of firms, providing an incentive for them to adopt best practices in addressing social and environmental issues that are inherent in their operations.

Companies, especially listed resources companies, are at the center of environmental controversies and of efforts to protect the interests of the communities within which they are operating. For multinational companies, especially resources companies, this poses more of a challenge. As leading Chinese resources companies have recently begun to expand abroad, their management of CSR issues in host communities across different countries is a challenge; but it is too soon to draw conclusions about this matter and further monitoring of the CSR performance of Chinese companies operating outside of China will be required.

SOCIAL ISSUES

Corporate social responsibility to employees in China is also very complex given its unique social and economic context. In the past 50 years, the government's heavy involvement in economic life through SOEs helped it to provide so-called "cradle-to-grave" social services to employees of SOEs, a system once known as the "iron rice bowl." For those publicly listed companies that are former SOEs, it is likely that these lifetime work practices will be maintained for some time in China; this is because China has adopted a gradualist, rather than a drastic approach, to reform. There are, however, signs of change as listed state-owned companies are slowly migrating to a system that transfers their responsibility to provide pensions to its employees to the governmental social security system in China.

Unions and Workers

As discussed in Chapter 4, in SOEs, unions were established by the government and union leaders were appointed by government. However, in most listed companies that are former SOEs, the union is still more or less controlled by government. The effectiveness of the union's role in these companies is doubtful, as under China's gradualist approach to economic reform, the government retains power to intervene in enterprise management systems, including the power to appoint union leaders. In most cases, a union leader is also a member of the ruling Communist Party.

Recent developments in regard to trade unions in China have shown that the passive role played by a nominated trade union member in corporate governance may well change in the near future. In May 2005, it was announced that the workers in one of China's largest steel companies, Panzihua Iron & Steel Group, were allowed to directly elect their leaders (People's Daily Online, 2005d). This appears to be an early step in a movement to reduce government administrative power in listed companies. However, one should be cautious about generalizing too much from isolated examples such as this.

CONCLUSION

Overall, CSR in China is still an emerging concept and it will take some time for it to gain wider acceptance. Nevertheless, the government's requirement that companies report on their CSR practices will no doubt help to promote greater awareness of this idea. Furthermore, we have seen that large resources companies in China are already taking a lead in following global standards and adopting good CSR practices. As these Chinese companies grow bigger and expand their practices abroad, their CSR practices will be put under greater scrutiny. This will create further challenges for these companies, but, unfortunately, this is a matter that cannot be pursued further here.

8   Resources Security and Corporate Governance

In a keynote speech at the Sustainability Business Conference for China and the UK given in London on April 15, 2008, The Rt. Hon. John Hutton MP, Secretary of State for Business, Enterprise and Regulatory Reform, pointed out that:

> Energy is once again a major issue on the international stage. Competition over access to, and control over energy resources is intensifying and coupled with the urgency of climate change presents a clear challenge to global energy systems. (Hutton, 2008)

The previous chapters have illustrated the important role of government in the development of corporate governance and the impact of corporate social responsibility (CSR) on leading resources companies in China. Given the growing economic power of China and the rise of its resources companies in recent years, it is appropriate to ask if China's aggressive attempt to control natural resources worldwide through its government-controlled resources companies will pose a threat to the world economy and stability. We can only hope to begin to answer this question here.

ECONOMIC GROWTH IN CHINA— A NEW THREAT TO RESOURCE SECURITY?

In the past 30 years, China's economy has grown at 8% per annum (Pukthuanthong and Walker, 2007) and could arguably maintain high levels of growth for the next 20 years (Zweig and Bi, 2005). This phenomenal growth has also put an upward demand pressure on natural resources. China has gradually grown from one of the largest energy exporting countries to a net energy importing country (Andrews-Speed, 2004). From 2000 to 2005, China's energy consumption grew at an average speed of 9.5% per year (Lin et al., 2006); by 2020, China could at least experience a two-fold increase in its energy consumption (Zhou et al., 2003).[1] This dramatic increase in demand for energy needs to be supported by the import of natural resources from resource-rich countries.

With China's growth in economic power and its increasing reliance on the import of natural resources to sustain its economic growth, maintaining access to valuable and scarce natural resources has emerged as being of the foremost importance for China. In China's latest White Paper on energy conditions and policies issued on December 26, 2007, China emphasized its need to rely on international cooperation to maintain stable energy supplies (Information Office of the State Council of the People's Republic of China, 2007: 19):

> China has forged increasingly closer ties with the outside world in the field of energy. . . . China has established a mechanism for dialogue and cooperation in the field of energy with a number of energy consuming and producing countries, such as the US, Japan and Russia, and the European Union . . . and has had extensive dialogues and exchanges with them in such aspects as energy policy and information data.

Furthermore, China has also "expanded its traditional relationship" with resource-rich developing countries such as Iran, Algeria, Egypt and Gabon (Zweig and Bi, 2005: 29). China's influence, and its far reaching policy on securing natural resources and sustaining its economic growth, has re-ignited concerns about global resource security.

History illustrates that competition for scarce natural resources, especially oil resources, often leads to resource wars, either among conflicting political forces within a particular country (Ross, 2004; Le Billon, 2005), or "it may encourage a foreign country to start or support a civil war" (Ross, 2004: 344). This can be demonstrated by oil conflicts in the Persian Gulf, energy conflicts in the Caspian Sea Basin, and oil wars in the South China Sea (Klare, 2001b). As one of the major energy consumers, the US became involved in various resource-related conflicts in order to maintain its energy supply, which seems critical to maintaining its economic growth (Klare, 2001b).

In the White Paper on energy conditions and policies, the PRC government emphasized that "China did not, does not and will not pose any threat to the world's energy security" (Information Office of the State Council of the People's Republic of China, 2007: 22). While China has committed itself to not threatening world peace, it would be wise to closely monitor Chinese policies and actions in conflict-ridden resource-rich countries. Indeed, China has already started working with resources-sector companies across the world through economic cooperation such as trade and direct investment.

In 2005, the China National Offshore Oil Corporation's (CNOOC) takeover bid for the US oil company Unocal was criticized by the US House of Representatives as a potential threat to national security (Zweig and Bi, 2005). However, this has not dampened Chinese interest in acquiring assets in the resources sector. In May 2007, China acquired a 10% interest in a private equity player—Blackstone (Dunstan, 2007)—and expected to gain indirect control of natural resources through this strategic investment. This time, the Chinese chose to be a non-voting shareholder so as to avoid encountering further opposition in the US based on 'national security' grounds (Markoff, 2007).

On the other hand, compared with the US, Australia does not seem to be as concerned with the so-called notion of "national interest." Not only have Chinese companies "quietly staked their claim on Australia's iron ore reserves" in the past 20 years (Zonneveldt, 2007: 1), recently Australia has also directly engaged with the state-owned Chinese resources companies in various resources projects. In August 2007, CNOOC was awarded its first permit to explore for oil and gas in Australian waters (Wilson, 2007), and China's state-owned SinoSteel may become one of the biggest uranium explorers in Australia (Zonneveldt, 2007). Overall, Chinese acquisitions of interests in Australia's mining and energy sector have increased from $62 million in 2006 to $1.8 billion in 2007. By April 2008, it had already jumped to $15.8 billion (Hyland, 2008).

Recent talks between the Chinese state-owned company ChemChina and Nufarm (an Australian pesticides maker) may be a test for these 'national security' concerns (Maiden, 2007); in the USA, these concerns defeated the CNOOC bid for Unocal in 2005. As long as the business world still welcomes Chinese investment and assuming that Australia's Rudd government "will not stand in the way of more aggressive Chinese investment in Australia" (Korporaal, 2007: 1), this increasing cooperation between the resources sectors in China and Australia is unlikely to change much in the near future.

Not only has China started to acquire resources assets in Australia, it has also started to grow its resources assets worldwide (Callick, 2006a). In November 2006, China signed an agreement with Petronas (owned by the Malaysian government) to supply Shanghai with liquefied natural gas for 25 years (Callick, 2006b). Another gas agreement was made in 2006 with Iran through the state-controlled Chinese company Sinopec (Callick, 2006c). Recently, CNOOC also looked at possible oil acquisitions in Africa, Southeast Asia and the Middle East (Bloomberg, 2007: 53), and China's leading coal producer, Shenhua Energy, is said to be considering taking over Indonesia's second largest coal producer, PT Adaro Indonesia (Reuters, 2007: 53).

The recent increase in Chinese investment in overseas resources projects seems in line with the recent White Paper on energy conditions and policies issued by the Chinese government. As stated in this White Paper, China will in the future also pursue more opportunities (through its SOEs) to obtain direct control of world natural resources in an effort to help China to stabilize its supply:

China supports direct overseas investment by *domestic qualified enterprises* to engage in transnational operation, and encourage such enterprises to participate in international energy cooperation and in the construction of overseas energy infrastructure . . . (emphasis added) (Information Office of the State Council of the People's Republic of China, 2007: 21)

These "domestic qualified enterprises" include the Chinese leading resources companies that are the subject in this book; this further illustrates the importance of understanding the corporate governance practices of these enterprises.

CORPORATE GOVERNANCE IN LEADING RESOURCES COMPANIES IN CHINA AND RESOURCES SECURITY

The phenomenal growth of China's economy has seen a dramatic increase in demand for natural resources, especially in the past ten years. Being one of the world's leading resource-consuming countries, the US has also closely watched the development of China and its demand for natural resources. More than a decade ago, a study sponsored by the US Department of Energy concluded that despite rapid economic growth in China and the accelerating speed with which the demand for natural resources has increased, only oil was seen as being likely to have an impact on resource security in the US (McCreary, 1996).

Following the recent attempt by a Chinese company to take over a major US oil company, as well as various deals that have been made with leading resources companies in Australia, the issue of resource security needs to be re-analyzed. China's unique status and its political relationship with the US is still of major concern internationally. While pursuing economic reform under its "socialist market economy," China is still perceived to be a country that could potentially pose a security threat to the US. With a fast-growing China and its ever-increasing economic power, China has sought to advance its national interest and in so doing it has gradually evolved to become a major player in international affairs. The current world financial crisis has only strengthened China's powerful position.

It is in China's national interest to acquire resources-producing assets across the world so as to reduce its reliance on the continuous supply of natural resources from developed countries. Having reigned in control over its 'national champions', including major resources companies, China's government is engaged in acquiring resources-sector assets across both the developed and developing world through its leading resources companies. Empirical evidence supports this; as illustrated in the previous section, China's leading resources companies are indeed being used as vehicles to pursue control of key resources assets in the global market. As long as the Chinese economy maintains its current level of growth, the quest for natural resources across the world to satisfy its energy needs will remain intense.

In addition to the activities of governments, leading resources companies are increasingly playing an important role in maintaining global resource security. Multinational resources companies have established significant operations across continents, which enable them to exert their influence worldwide. The proposed merger between BHP Billiton and Rio Tinto, might have created a massive organization with enormous economies of scale and negotiating power; it could also potentially adversely affect major iron ore customers of Rio Tinto and BHP Billiton, such as China's steel mills (de Kretser, 2007). The possibility of a counter bid by a Chinese consortium would certainly raise concerns not just on the issues of fairness (as it was argued that the Chinese state-owned companies have more access to cheaper funds and are less transparent than their Western counterparts); it could also once again raise the issue of 'national interest', which would be considered by the Australian Treasurer, on advice from the Foreign Investment Review Board (Tingle, 2007). This became evident after the Chinese resources company, Chinalco, sought to acquire an 18% stake in Rio Tinto.

The sheer economic power of such resources companies, therefore, makes their governance a pivotal issue for study. As demonstrated in previous chapters, China's leading resources companies are under tight control from their government. Because China is still developing its socialist market economy with its tight government controls, the corporate governance of listed resources-sector companies is inevitably intertwined with public sector governance in China.

The worldwide acquisition of resources assets will no doubt see Chinese governance practices being put under more scrutiny by the outside world. On the other hand, in cooperating with the world's leading resources companies, Chinese listed companies will also be subject to the influence of the "best practices" in governance found in these leading Western companies. It would be interesting to see if these could serve as a vehicle for Chinese companies to learn from the West by adopting these "best practices"; this not only applies to narrow governance issues such as board management, but also to wider governance issues such as better environmental practices and providing better protection for employees.

The collapse of the Soviet Union and other Eastern European socialist countries has brought about fundamental shifts in world politics. Since then, 'cooperation' is probably mentioned more often than 'confrontation'. With further integration of the world economy and with the PRC being admitted to the World Trade Organization (WTO) in 2001, the geopolitical landscape has shifted dramatically from cold war to a new underlying economic war. Like the US, China will no doubt use its economic power to strengthening its global political influence.

The looming nature of competition for scarce natural resources has been widely discussed by political scientists (Klare, 2001b, a; Le Billon, 2005, 2001). Taking a more optimistic view, it is possible that the sovereign power embedded in SOEs will enable them to act as a catalyst for the transfer of best practices regarding wider governance issues (such as environmental and employee protection practices) to companies in less-developed countries. If China is able to achieve this, it will show that it has developed much greater sophistication in exerting its global influence.

9 Conclusions
Challenge for the Future

It doesn't matter if a cat is black or white, so long as it catches mice.

–Deng Xiaoping

Since the Chinese leader Deng Xiaoping made this famous quip 30 years ago, China has been on a transformative and challenging journey of social, economic and enterprise reform. Thirty years has witnessed remarkable progress in China. Not only has China become a leading emerging economy, it has also become an interesting research subject as it travelled along a unique road to building the so-called "socialist market economy."

The phenomenal growth of the Chinese economy in the past 30 years has witnessed the rise of internationally-active Chinese companies. While China has taken a gradualist approach to its economic and enterprise reforms, enterprises in China have also slowly gone through a dramatic transformation in the past 20 years, especially since the Shenzhen and Shanghai Stock Exchanges were established in 1990 and 1991, respectively.

Among the many things that we need to understand about China, the governance of listed companies remains an important area. Listed companies in China have gone through a process of transforming themselves from wholly state-owned enterprises into companies listed on stock exchanges but with government control through major holdings of non-tradable shares. Since 2005, listed companies have also undergone another major reform, which was to convert the non-tradable shares held by the government into tradable shares. This reform aimed to bring more transparency to the share ownership structure of companies in order to facilitate better corporate governance practices.

The remarkable economic growth that China has undergone also saw the rise of its leading resources companies. These Chinese resources companies have become well known worldwide. This has sometimes led to controversy, such as with the proposed takeover of the US oil company Unocal by the China National Offshore Oil Corporation (CNOOC). At other times this international growth has been relatively uneventful, as reflected in the co-operation between major steel makers in China and Australian iron ore suppliers. Despite their new status in the world economy, the corporate governance practices of China's resources companies remain less well understood than they should be by the outside world.

To help us understand the governance practices of listed companies in China, this book has reported on detailed research on corporate governance at leading resources companies. Interviews with regulators, legal professionals, corporate governance experts and controllers of leading resources companies have provided insights on how these companies are managed and governed. This book has sought to begin to fill gaps in our knowledge of this sector by providing a detailed analysis of corporate governance in these leading Chinese companies and has also provided comparisons with corporate governance practices in comparable world leading resources companies including BHP Billiton, Rio Tinto, Shell and Chevron.

Despite the economic and enterprise reforms that have occurred since 1978, China's listed companies are still more or less controlled by government. As a sector of strategic importance and national significance, resources companies remain under tight control of government. This suggests that corporate governance and public sector governance in China will be closely intertwined for some time yet.

In 2002, the China Securities and Regulatory Commission introduced 'The code of corporate governance for listed companies in China'. Apart from appointing independent directors to their boards, since the passage of the PRC Company Law in December 1993, listed companies in China have also been required to establish a supervisory board. While these new rules and regulations have helped with establishing a systematic governance system for listed companies in China (as we saw in our discussion of listed resources companies), government, as a major shareholder of leading companies, still appoints directors (including independent directors) and supervisors to the boards and supervisory boards of major companies.

Specifically, in terms of the corporate governance practices of leading resources companies, the PRC government is not only the major shareholder in most of these companies, it also appoints the chairman and its directors and, through the Party, plays a major role in the appointment of all key company officers. The government also exerts its controlling power through the appointment of the head of the sub-branch of the Communist Party in all resources companies. This has inevitably raised concerns about the effectiveness of some governance practices.

Other issues that have attracted public attention include the handling of related party transactions and the protection of minority shareholder interests. These issues are further complicated by the fact that when most listed companies were first listed, the government had chosen to package the best assets from former state-owned enterprises (in order to ensure their successful listing). Consequently, most listed companies still have numerous business and social ties with other companies in the group that the listed company is part of. In addition, major listed companies (as is the case in leading resources companies) still have a state-owned company as its controlling shareholder.

Since 2005, the unequal status of tradable and government-owned shares, has been gradually remedied. As more shares became tradable, it will be interesting to see how much the share ownership structure in China will evolve and whether it could lead to better protection of minority shareholder interests and the improvement on board performance in the longer term.

The economic development of China has also imposed a heavy cost on the environment. Research shows that environmental damage will not only slow economic growth in China, it has already heavily affected health and well-being of its population (Chan et al., 2008; OECD, 2007; Economy, 2004).

In 2008, concerned by the environmental, social and governance costs that economic development had imposed on the wider society, the government (through SASAC) started to promote corporate social responsibility (CSR) practices through more stringent reporting requirements of listed companies. For resources companies, the extractive nature of their businesses means that these companies will have a more dramatic impact on the environment and that there is more environmental risk associated with their operations. The need to report on CSR practices will encourage resources companies to observe best practices in the industry; it will also help to make these companies more transparent on CSR issues and further help investors to better understand the risks associated with CSR. In fact, one of the leading resources companies, Sinopec, has already started to report its environmental and social practices following international best practice—the Global Reporting Initiative (SIRAN, 2008).

Resource security is another issue that needs to be monitored closely as China's resources companies are also tools of government in regard to this broader geopolitical agenda. From the Chinese government's point of view, being a major shareholder of resources companies allows the government to control natural resources abroad by employing market mechanisms such as takeovers and mergers. The issue of resource security is further complicated as governments can use market mechanisms to exert their economic influence while avoiding direct political confrontation.

In 2005, the potential takeover of Unocal by CNOOC sparked national security concerns in the US (Zweig and Bi, 2005). On the other hand, Australia seems not as concerned about such matters. Recently, the Australian Government Foreign Investment Review Board cleared the way for Chinalco (100% owned by the Chinese government) to acquire 14.99% of Rio Tinto plc (equalling about 11% of the dual-listed company), as long as Chinalco did not seek to appoint a director to the company (Taylor, 2008). However, Chinalco subsequently sought in vain to strengthen its position as Rio Tinto has sought to raise additional capital to meet its obligations.

Thirty years of economic and enterprise reform has transformed China from a stagnant planned economy into a leading economic powerhouse in the world. In recent years, Chinese resources companies have attracted more public attention given their phenomenal economic growth following the upward trajectory of growth in China. Nevertheless, China faces challenges to improve its environmental, and its social and governance practices and at the same time to maintain its economic growth.

The complexity of the current governance system combined with the gradualist approach taken by the government in its social and economic reforms indicates that it will take some time for China to reform its current system. Nevertheless, the intertwining of corporate governance with government administrative measures suggests that the government can be very influential in guiding listed companies. High volatility in the Chinese stock market[1] in recent years has seen many investors suffer huge losses. Improving corporate governance will help to restore investor confidence and foster further development of the stock market in China.

While it is a good sign that the government has started promoting CSR reporting in early 2008, it is important that listed companies further improve their CSR practices. Given the high-risk nature of the resources sector and the rapid growth and expansion of China's resources companies, dealing with CSR issues remains a major challenge. Resources companies are at the center of the debate concerning the critical issue of climate change; the CSR practices of these companies will not only affect the future sustainable development of the world, they will also have obvious political significance given that the Chinese government plays such a central role behind all these companies.

Furthermore, companies that incorporate good CSR practices in their operations will be seen as being more attractive to investors, especially to those who have signed the Principles for Responsible Investment (PRI). This could, therefore, potentially attract more quality investors.

In addition, the resources industry is also facing pressure from society to supply critical energy needs at a reasonable cost and to minimize disruptive costs to the environment. This will continue to create major challenges for the next 10 or 20 years. It will take substantial co-operation between corporations and the societies in which they operate to solve this problem. This will be a greater challenge for leading Chinese companies as they seek to further expand overseas and to observe international standards (or best practices) in the regions in which they operate. The capabilities of these companies will partly depend on the integrity of their corporate governance structures and the capacity of their management structure to ensure transparency and accountability.

Given these challenges, the further development of China's major resources companies needs to be closely studied. Further research focusing on CSR and resource security will help to build better understanding of these companies and of the challenges that they face. Such research will also be important to policy makers around the world especially those dealing extensively with Chinese companies. We are just beginning to see the size of this problem.

Notes

NOTES TO CHAPTER 1

1. The Chinese "legal person" entity can be traced to the 1993 Company Law: a "limited liability company" or "joint stock limited company" is an enterprise legal person (lexmercatoria.org, 1997: 1).
2. Ironically, sometimes, the control by the government can also adversely affect share performance. For example, recently, PetroChina lost two-thirds of its peak value since it was listed in the A-share market in November 2007, as the government did not allow the company to raise retail gasoline prices to be in line with the international oil price (Garnaut, 2008).
3. The original text is in Chinese and it was translated by Xinting Jia.
4. The original text is in Chinese and it was translated by Xinting Jia.
5. The original text is in Chinese and it was translated by Xinting Jia.
6. The original text is in Chinese and was translated by Xinting Jia.
7. In 2005, when the share split structure reform was started, in order to maintain the stability of the stock market, it was required by the government that the reform plan must include a lock-up period of 24–36 months before the non-tradable shares become tradable on the market. Now more than two years have passed, most companies have passed the lock-up period, hence the concern.
8. There are a number of shares issued by Chinese listed companies. 'A-share' refers to the type of common share that was issued in China's domestic share market and quoted in RMB, and previously was only available to domestic investors.

NOTES TO CHAPTER 2

1. Based on an interview with a company secretary. Because of the confidential agreement with the interviewee, the name of the person and his (her) affiliated organization cannot be disclosed here.
2. Available in Chinese: http://www.cet.com.cn/20041122/YAOWEN/200411223.htm
3. The original is in Chinese, the translation is by Xinting Jia.
4. Not all National State-owned Enterprises are listed.
5. The original text is in Chinese and this was translated into English by Xinting Jia.
6. The original was in Chinese, the English translation was by Xinting Jia.
7. Based on the view of company secretaries and government officials interviewed by the authors.
8. Based on the view of company secretaries and government officials interviewed by the authors.
9. Based on the view of company secretaries and government officials interviewed by the authors.

10. The "one country, two systems" existing in mainland China and Hong Kong means that companies listed in Hong Kong are not regulated by the CSRC and only need to abide by the listing requirements of the Hong Kong Stock Exchange.
11. All the 74 companies' 2002 annual reports are in Chinese.
12. TCL Communications Equipment Corporation Limited is listed on the Shanghai Stock Exchange and ranked number 22 on the *Fortune* top 100 China list.
13. The original text is in Chinese and the English translation is by Xinting Jia.

NOTES TO CHAPTER 3

1. According to Hobbs (2000), in 1999, institutional investors owned about 58% of equity in the top 1000 companies in the US.
2. Banks in the US cannot hold more than 5% of a single company under American laws (Kanda, 1998: 929).
3. This English-version categorization follows Tong (2005).
4. Section 9 of Corporations Act 2001 provides further explanation of the meaning of a substantial shareholding.
5. Rio Tinto is a dual-listed company and is listed on the London Stock Exchange (as Rio Tinto plc) and on the Australia Stock Exchange (as Rio Tinto Ltd.).
6. As CNOOC is not domestically listed in China, being listed only offshore, it does not need to establish a supervisory board.
7. CNOOC is not domestically listed in China; it is only listed offshore. Therefore, it does not need to establish a supervisory board.
8. The New York Stock Exchange listing rules require that board committees should be set up by listed companies. The board committees are also recommended by the Code of Corporate Governance for Listed Companies in China issued by CSRC.

NOTES TO CHAPTER 4

1. Most material in the chapter is based on interviews conducted in mainland China and Hong Kong in 2004 for the Australian Research Council (ARC)-sponsored research project: "Directing the top 100 companies: corporate governance and corporate law in the top 100 companies in China." The list of the top 100 companies is the list published by *Fortune* magazine in 2004 and is the list from which the ten leading resources companies studied in this book are selected. The project leaders were Professors Roman Tomasic, Neil Andrews and Dr. Jane Fu. Dr. Xinting Jia was a team member of this project. Overall, more than 100 interviews were conducted, and most interviewees answered interview questions in Mandarin Chinese and the answers were later translated into English. Altogether, 29 of these interviews (with government officials and controllers of leading resources companies) were used to write this chapter.
    Also see further Tomasic, R. and Andrews, N. 2007, Minority shareholder protection in China's top 100 listed companies. *Australian Journal of Asian Law*, vol. 9, no. 1, pp. 88–119; Tomasic, R. and Jian, F. U. 2006, Legal regulation and corporate governance in China's top 100 listed companies. *The Company Lawyer*, vol. 27, no. 9, pp. 278–287; Andrews, N. and Tomasic, R. 2006, Directing China's top 100 listed companies: corporate governance in an emerging market economy. *The Corporate Governance Law Review*, vol. 2, no. 3, pp. 245–309.
2. For further details, please refer to Chapter 2.
3. These six companies are Sinopec (China Petroleum & Chemical Corporation), PetroChina, Minmetals Development, Baoshan Iron & Steel, CNOOC and Aluminum Corporation of China.

4. Sinopec Shanghai is a subsidiary of Sinopec.
5. In Article 20 of the PRC Company Law (final revision issued on October 27, 2005; a Chinese version may be available at http://www.csrc.gov.cn), it stipulates that the shareholders of the company must abide by the law, administrative regulation and company's articles of association to fulfil their responsibilities as shareholders. The shareholders of the company must not misuse their shareholder's position to exploit the interests of the company as well as the interests of other shareholders.
6. Part 2D.6 of the Australian Corporations Act 2001 provides for the disqualification of persons, such as directors and managers, from involvement in managing a corporation. A person so disqualified is prohibited from managing a corporation. Disqualification will arise automatically in certain circumstances under sections 206B and 206C (e.g, conviction for a criminal offence, bankruptcy and contravention of a civil penalty order); disqualification will also occur where an officer of a company has repeatedly contravened the Corporations Act (s 206E). ASIC has power to disqualify a person from managing a corporation for up to five years if they have been an officer or director of two or more companies that have gone into liquidation in the previous seven years, provided that certain safeguards are met under s 206F. Persons who have been disqualified under any of the above provisions may apply to the court to be allowed to manage a corporation once again, but these applications will be considered very closely under s 206G.
7. All the shares held by the state are non-tradable, therefore making this figure relatively stable and still valid. Although China started to tackle the non-tradable shares problem in May 2005, the slow pace of the reform will render the current share ownership structure relatively stable for the near future.
8. More about this matter is discussed in Chapter 6.
9. CNOOC is only listed in overseas stock exchanges; therefore, it is not regulated by the CSRC.

NOTES TO CHAPTER 5

1. This is partly due to the spin-off of BHP Steel as a separate entity, which was renamed as Bluescope Steel.
2. This conclusion was reached by Xinting Jia from personal experience gained by working at BHP Billiton global headquarters at 600 Bourke Street, Melbourne, Australia from March 2001 to March 2002.
3. The rating summary was available at http://www.reputex.com.au/pdfs/2003Summary_split/bhp.pdf.
4. ISO 14001 is the international standard for environmental management systems and covers the general requirements, implementation and operation and checking and corrective actions for environmental management systems (Standards Australia, 1996).
5. Rio Tinto's shareholding structure received an unexpected jolt in 2008 when the leading Chinese government controlled aluminium company, Chinalco, acquired a 9% stake in the Rio Tino group, becoming its largest shareholder. This occurred at a time when concerns had been expressed in China about the now abandoned attempted takeover of Rio Tinto by BHP Limited, which would have led to further concentration in the resources sector. Chinalco subsequently sought to increase its shareholdings in Rio Tinto to 18% and to seek two board seats on the Rio board as part of a $19.5 billion deal with Rio aimed at easing Rio's debt burdens. In 2008 Chinalco had suggested that it would not seek to acquire more than 14.9% of Rio and not seek to board positions in the company, but the proposed new deal would go beyond this. This generated a popular political outcry in Australia and a shareholder backlash in the United Kingdom

by shareholders who complained that their pre-emptive rights had been trampled upon. In early June 2009, Rio Tinto decided to abandon this agreement and make alternative arrangements for dealing with its debt situation. Unfortunately, it is not possible to discuss these matters in any detail here; but see further: Fletcher, R., 'Chinalco rules out bigger stake in Rio Tinto, *The Daily Telegraph*, 5 February 2008; White, G., 'Rio Tinto faces political headwinds in Australia', *The Daily Telegraph*, 18 March 2009; Webb, T. and Finch, J., 'Rio Shareholders rebel over Chinalco bail-out', *The Guardian*, 13 February 2009 at p. 31; Smith, P., 'Chinalco recasts Rio investment in effort to win over shareholders', *The Financial Times*, 22 May 2009 at p 15. Also see: Wilson, A, 'Chinalco chairman in Australia to discuss Rio deal', *The Australian*, 4 June 2009; Chambers, M, 'Bye Bye Beijing, hello BHP', *The Australian*, 6 June 2009; Macnamara, W., 'The last rites are said after deal runs out of friends', *The Financial Times*, 5 June 2009 at p 19; Macalister, T, 'Rio Tinto rights issue imminent after controversial Chinalco deal collapses', *The Guardian*, 5 June 2009 at p 28.

6. These reports may be available at http://www.riotinto.com/investor/information/socrecinv/reporting.aspx.
7. The rating summary was available at http://www.reputex.com.au/pdfs/2003Summary_split/riotinto.pdf.
8. These reports may be available at http://www.riotinto.com/investor/information/socrecinv/reporting.aspx.

NOTES TO CHAPTER 6

1. This is calculated at exchange rate AUD\$1 = RMB¥6.
2. Sinopec is listed in New York as ADR (American Depositary Receipts).
3. There are many characteristics related to the unique Chinese model; one already discussed is the unique ownership structure of Sinopec, with more than 50% of its shares being non-tradable.
4. The abolition of Ministry of Chemical Industry is part of China's revamping the ministries in 1998, which is also an essential part of China's recent economic and enterprise reform.
5. According to Nolan (2001: 54), the massive restructuring included China National Petrochemical Corporation transferring 19 petrochemical enterprises to China National Petroleum Corporation; and China National Petroleum Corporations transferring 12 companies to China National Petrochemical Corporation in order to restructure them as two vertically integrated oil and petrochemical groups.
6. http://english.sinopec.com/en-company/en-subsidiaries/index.shtml.
7. Original data is in Chinese and is available from the Baosteel's website.
8. The original text is in Chinese; it was translated by Xinting Jia.

NOTES TO CHAPTER 8

1. See Zhou et al., 2003; the two-fold increase in energy consumption was indeed a very conservative estimation, which was based on the Chinese government adopting aggressive policies to achieve greater energy efficiency and switch to cleaner fuels.

NOTES TO CHAPTER 9

1. In the past two years, the Shanghai Composite Index reached as high as 6124 points. On September 5, 2008, it had fallen to 2200 points.

References

Adams, K. 2004. *Five steps to engage the Dragon: the challenges for Australian manufacturing in the Chinese century.* Available: http://www.bluescopesteel. com, accessed May 11, 2005.

Alkhafaji, A. F. 1989. *A stakeholder approach to corporate governance: managing in a dynamic environment.* Quorum Books, New York.

Andrews-Speed, P. 2004. *Energy policy and regulation in the People's Republic of China,* Kluwer Law International, New York.

Anonymous 1. *"Jiuwu" dangan: cong "yiwu" dao "jiuwu" (Nine five-year plans: from the first five-year plan to the ninth five-year plan).* Available: http://www. china.org.cn/ch-15/15/b.htm, accessed August 16, 2004.

Anonymous 2. *Woguo liuge wunian jihua (Six five-year plans of China).* Available: http://wlzx.hdpu.edu.cn/upc/hongqi/dshx/025.htm, accessed August 16, 2004.

Anonymous 2002. *Guanyu Kaizhan Shangshi Gongsi Jianli Xiandai Qiye Zhidu Jiancha de Tongzhi.* Available: http://news.xinhuanet.com/zhengfu/2002–05/13/content_390389.htm, accessed August 23, 2004.

Aoki, M. 2000. *Information, corporate governance, and institutional diversity: competitiveness in Japan, the USA, and the transitional economies.* Oxford University Press, Oxford.

Armour, J. and McCahery, J. A. (eds.) 2006. *After Enron: improving corporate law and modernising securities regulation in Europe and the US.* Hart Publishing, Oxford.

Ashworth, J. 2004. Hands-on man at the helm. *The Australian,* August 30, 2004, p. 42.

Asian Development Bank 2005. *Making profits, protecting our planet: Asian environment outlook 2005.* Available: http://www.adb.org/Documents/Books/ AEO/2005/aeo-2005.pdf, accessed January 27, 2008.

ASIC 2004. *How do dual listed companies work?* Available: http://www.asic.gov. au/fido/fido.nsf/byheadline/How+do+dual+listed+companies+work%3F?opend ocument, accessed September 20, 2004.

ASX Corporate Governance Council 2007. *Corporate governance principles and recommendations, 2nd version.* Available: http://www.asx.com.au/supervision/ governance/Revised_Corporate_Governance_Principles_and_Recommenda-tions.htm, accessed October 10, 2007.

Australian Mines and Metals Association 2001. *Australian resources sector: the case for ongoing flexibility in employment arrangement options.* Available: http://www.amma.org.au/publications/Australian%20resources%20sector. pdf, accessed January 30, 2005.

Australian Mines and Metals Association 2004. *The case for ongoing flexibility in employment arrangement options in the Australian resources sector.* Available:

http://www.amma.org.au/tl_index_publications.html, accessed January 30, 2005.

Australian Stock Exchange 2003. *ASX listed companies as at Sat March 15 00:25:24 GMT+11:00 2003*. Available: http://www.asx.com.au/asx/research/CompanyListed.jsp, accessed March 15, 2003.

Bakan, J. 2004. *The corporation: the pathological pursuit of profit and power*. Free Press, New York.

Baker, J., Baker, L., Nadi, S., Ng, P. and Kaseman, P. 2002. The top 500. *Business Review Weekly*, vol. 24, no. 16, April 24, 2002, pp. 64–74.

Baker, L., Curtain, R., Nadarajah, S. and Ng, P. 2003. The top 500. *Business Review Weekly*, vol. 25, no. 15, April 24, 2003, pp. 64–73.

Baldauf, S. 1998. Lone star lawsuit takes on oil giants. *Christian Science Monitor*, vol. 90, no. 105, pp. 1.

Bandrapalli, S. 1996. Shell oil still wrestles with problem: what do with old, rusty oil rig? *Christian Science Monitor*, vol. 88, no. 131, pp. 18.

Baoshan Iron & Steel Co., Ltd. 2003. *Baoshan Iron & Steel Co., Ltd. Annual Report 2003*. Available: http://www.baosteel.com/, accessed January 26, 2006.

Baoshan Iron & Steel Co., Ltd. 2004. *Baoshan Iron & Steel Co., Ltd. Annual Report 2004*. Available: http://www.baosteel.com/, accessed January 26, 2006.

Baoshan Iron & Steel Co., Ltd. 2005a. *Baoshan Iron & Steel Interim Report 2005*. Available: http://www.baosteel.com/, accessed January 21, 2006.

Baoshan Iron & Steel Co., Ltd. 2005b. *Baoshan Iron & Steel Third-Quarter Report 2005*. Available: http://www.baosteel.com/, accessed January 20, 2006.

Baoshan Iron & Steel Co., Ltd. 2005c. *Overview of the company*. Available: http://www.baosteel.com/, accessed January 20, 2006.

Bartholomeusz, S. 2001. BHP Billiton merger is a match made in heaven. *The Sydney Morning Herald*, June 30, 2001, p. 50.

Barton, D. and Huang, R. H. 2007. *Governing China's board: an interview with John Thornton*. Available: http://unpan1.un.org/intradoc/groups/public/documents/APCITY/UNPAN027097.pdf, accessed June 1, 2008.

Bedi, J. and Tennant, P. 2002. *Dual-listed companies*. Available: http://www.rba.gov.au/PublicationsAndResearch/Bulletin/bu_oct02/bu_1002_2.pdf, accessed May 6, 2002.

Beesley, M. and Evans, T. 1978. *Corporate social responsibility: a reassessment*. Croom Helm Ltd., London.

Berle, A. A. 1932. For whom corporate managers are trustees: a note. *Harvard Law Review*, vol. 45, no. 7, pp. 1365–1372.

Berle, A. A. and Means, G. C. 1932. *The modern corporation and private property*. Macmillan, New York.

BHP Billiton 2001. *Financial statements BHP Billiton Limited*. Available: http://www.bhpbilliton.com/bbContentRepository/Reports/2001BHPBillitonLtdAnnualReport_partD.pdf, accessed September 20, 2004.

BHP Billiton 2004a. *BHP history*. Available: http://www.bhpbilliton.com/bb/aboutUs/companyOverview/ourHistory/bhpHistory.jsp, accessed September 17, 2004.

BHP Billiton 2004b. *Our structure*. Available: http://www.bhpbilliton.com.au/bb/aboutUs/companyOverview/ourStructure.jsp, accessed September 15, 2004.

BHP Billiton 2004c. *Working for a sustainable future: BHP Billiton health safety environment and community report full report 2004*. Available: http://hsecreport.bhpbilliton.com/2004/repository/feedback/bhpb_full_hsec_report.pdf, accessed October 4, 2004.

BHP Billiton 2007a. *Awards & Commendations*. Available: http://www.bhpbilliton.com/bb/sustainableDevelopment/2007AtAGlance/externalRecognition.jsp, accessed June 1, 2008.

BHP Billiton 2007b. *BHP Billiton 2007 sustainability report.* Available: http://www.bhpbilliton.com/bbContentRepository/200710338624/sustainabilityreport.pdf, accessed June 2, 2008.

BHP Billiton 2007c. *BHP Billiton annual report 2007.* Available: http://www.bhpbilliton.com/bb/investorsMedia/reports/2007/2007BhpBillitonAnnualReportPage.jsp, accessed June 1, 2008.

BHP Billiton 2008. *Global operations.* Available: http://www.bhpbilliton.com/bb/home.jsp, accessed May 11, 2008.

Bloomberg 2007. CNOOC on the prowl. *The Australian Financial Review,* November 2, 2007, p. 53.

BP plc 2004. *BP to sell equity stake in Sinopec.* Available: http://www.scandoil.com/moxie/business/money/bp-to-sell-equity-stake-i.shtml, accessed February 14, 2005.

Brahm, L. 2003. Zhu Rongji's "managed marketization" of the Chinese economy, in Mar, P. and Richter, F. (eds.) *China: enabling a new era of changes.* John Wiley & Sons (Asia), Singapore.

Broadman, H. G. 2001. *Lessons from corporatization and corporate governance reform in Russia and China,* World Bank. Available: http://www.developmentgateway.com/download/106673/Russia_vs_China_SOEs.pdf, accessed May 2, 2003.

Buhr, H. and Grafström, M. 2007. The making of meaning in the media: the case of corporate social responsibility in the Financial Times, in den Hond, F., de Bakker, F. G. A. and Neergaard, P. (eds.) *Managing corporate social responsibility in action.* Ashgate, Aldershot, pp. 15–31.

Burr, B. B. 2000. Labor digging at Rio Tinto. *Pensions & Investments,* vol. 28, no. 7, pp. 32.

Burrell, A. 2008. Crean may open door to Chinese money. *The Australian Financial Review,* April 21, 2008, p. 1, 4.

Burton, B. 2002. The big ugly at Ok Tedi. *Multinational Monitor,* January/February, pp. 6.

Business Week. 2005, The best Asian performers, October 24, p. 55.

Callick, R. 2001. Merger destined for world stage. *The Australian Financial Review,* May 19, 2001, p. 12.

Callick, R. 2006a. China Inc's global hunt. *The Australian,* September 16, 2006, p. 1, 36.

Callick, R. 2006b. Petronas in China gas deal. *The Australian,* November 1, 2006, p. 1, 39.

Callick, R. 2006c. Sinopec in $128bn Iran oil, gas deal. *The Australian,* November 20, 2006, pp. 1, 41.

Callick, R., Allen, L. and Power, B. 2002. $25bn deal boosts China ties. *The Australian Financial Review,* August 9, 2002, p. 1.

Carroll, A. B. and Buchholtz, A. K. 2003. *Business and society: ethics and stakeholder management,* 5th. South-Western, Mason, OH.

Chan, W.-S., Kruse, C., Li, S. and Singanayaga, B. 2008. *ESG in China: The issues, the effects and the cost to development.* Available: http://www.jpmorgan.com/pages/jpmorgan/investbk/solutions/research/climatechange, accessed September 7, 2008.

Chao, Y. 2007. *Abiding by international best practices: building a model for a harmonious and efficient board of directors for China Life.* Available: http://www.oecd.org/dataoecd/18/1/39305548.pdf, accessed May 31, 2008.

Charkham, J. P. 1995. *Keeping good company: a study of corporate governance in five countries.* Oxford University Press, Oxford.

Cheffins, B. R. 2002a. Comparative corporate governance and the Australian experience, in Ramsay, I. (ed.) *Key developments in corporate law and trusts law: essays in honour of Professor Harold Ford*. LexisNexis Butterworths, Sydney, pp. 13–38.

Cheffins, B. R. 2002b. Corporate governance convergence: lessons from Australia. *Transnational Lawyer*, vol. 16, pp. 13–43.

Chen, J. 1994. *From administrative authorisation to private law: a comparative perspective of the developing civil law in the People's Republic of China*. Martinus Nijhoff Publishers, Dordrecht.

Chen, K. 1998. China's revamped ministries expected to create huge new firms for listings. *The Wall Street Journal*, March 9, 1998, p. B11B.

Chen, M. and Florian, E. 2002. The China 100. *Fortune*, vol. 145, no. 2, pp. 34–36.

Chen, Z. 2004. *Fei Niao Jin, Liang Gong Cang: Duli Jianguan Jigou de Mingyun (The fate of the Independent Supervisory Institution)*. Available: http://www.asiatimes-chinese.com/2004/08/0818rep3.htm, accessed September 4, 2004.

Chevron 2007. *Investing in human energy: 2006 corporate responsibility report*. Available: http://www.chevron.com/GlobalIssues/CorporateResponsibility/2006/documents/2006_chevron_crr.pdf, accessed March 24, 2008.

Chevron 2008a. *Company profile*. Available: http://www.chevron.com/about/leadership/, accessed March 2, 2008.

Chevron 2008b. *Organization chart*. Available: http://www.chevron.com/about/leadership/organizationchart/, accessed March 23, 2008.

ChevronToxico 2005. *Chevron's rainforest Chernobyl*. Available: http://chevrontoxico.com/downloads/OnepagercasesummaryFINAL.doc, accessed March 24, 2008.

China Knowledge Press 2005, *Financial services in China: the past, present and future of a changing industry*. China Knowledge Press, Singapore.

China Online 2000. *China Securities Regulatory Commission (CSRC): organizational profile*. Available: http://www.chinaonline.com/refer/ministry_profiles/CSRC.asp, accessed September 4, 2004.

China Securities Regulatory Commission 2001. *Guidelines for introducing independent directors to the board of directors of listed companies*. Available: http://www.csrc.gov.cn, accessed August 30, 2004.

China Securities Regulatory Commission 2002. *Code of corporate governance for listed companies in China*. Available: http://www.csrc.gov.cn/, accessed February 27, 2004.

China Securities Regulatory Commission and People's Bank of China 2002. *Provisional measures on administration of domestic securities investments of Qualified Foreign Institutional Investors(QFII)*. Available: http://www.csrc.gov.cn/en/jsp/detail.jsp?infoid=1061947782100&type=CMS.STD, accessed May 23, 2005.

CNNMoney.com 2008. *Fortune Global 500*. Available: http://money.cnn.com/magazines/fortune/global500/2007/snapshots/10694.html, accessed June 15, 2008.

Cohen, M. 1996. Murder in Nigeria. *Canadian Dimension*, vol. 30, no. 3, pp. 45–49.

CSRC 2005. *Administrative measures on the split share structure reform of listed companies*. Available: http://www.csrc.gov.cn, accessed January 7, 2006.

CSRC, MOF and SETC 2002. *Circular on issues and associated with the sale of state-owned shares and legal person shares of listed companies to foreign investors*. Available: http://www.setc.gov.cn/dwjxycybh/200211130019.htm, accessed July 31, 2005.

CSRC and SASAC 2003. *Circular on certain issues relating to fund transfer between listed company and their related parties and guarantees provided by listed companies*. Available: http://www.mofcom.gov.cn/, accessed July 31, 2005.

CSRC, SASAC, Ministry of Finance, People's Bank of China and Ministry of Commerce 2005. *Guidance on reforming split share ownership structure in listed* companies *(guanyu shangshi gongsi guquan fenzhi gaige de zhidao yijian)*. Available: http://www.csrc.gov.cn, accessed January 7, 2006.

Cummins, I. and Beasant, J. 2005. *Shell shock: the secrets and spin of an oil giant.* Mainstream Publishing Company, Edinburgh.

Dahya, J., Karbhari, Y., Xiao, J. Z. and Yang, M. 2003. The usefulness of the supervisory board report in China. *Corporate Governance: An International Review,* vol. 11, no. 4, pp. 308–321.

de Kretser, A. 2007. Baosteel stirs Rio Tinto pot. *The Australian Financial Review,* December 5, 2007, p. 51.

DFAT 2008. *Australia-China Free Trade Agreement negotiations.* Available: http://www.dfat.gov.au/geo/china/fta/index.html, accessed May 25, 2008.

Dodd, E. M. 1932. For whom are corporate managers trustees? *Harvard Law Review,* vol. 45, no. 7, pp. 1145–1163.

Dolin, A. 2002. Boosting shareholder participation – how well do you know your investors?, available at: http://www-au.computershare.com/content/download. asp?docId=%7B863DED4E-1331-4FC1-97E7-ED99DF85C356%7D&cc=AU &lang=en&bhjs=1&fla=0&theme=cpu, accessed 7 July 2009.

du Plessis, J., Großfeld, B., Luttermann, C., Saenger, I. and Sandrock, O. 2007. *German corporate governance in international and European context.* Springer, Berlin.

Dunstan, B. 2007. New threat to resources. *The Australian Financial Review,* June 8, 2007, p. 32.

Duris, J. 2004. How BHP chief will earn his pay. *Australian Financial Review,* September 17, 2004, p. 84.

Economy, E. C. 2004. *The river runs black: the environmental challenge to China's future.* Cornell University Press, Ithaca.

Eisenberg, M. 1976. *The structure of the corporation: a legal analysis.* Little, Brown, Boston.

Equator Principles 2008. *The Equator Principles.* Available: http://www.equator-principles.com/, accessed January 28, 2008.

Farrar, J. H. 2005. *Corporate governance: theories, principles, and practice,* 2nd. Oxford University Press, Melbourne.

FitzGerald, B. 2003. Business—Rio Tinto to end double posts. *The Sydney Morning Herald,* April 9, 2003, p. 22.

Fortune China 2004. Zhongguo Shangshi Gongsi 100 qiang (The top 100 listed companies in China). *Fortune China,* vol. 67, pp. 52–57.

Franks, J. and Mayer, C. 1997. Corporate ownership and control in the U.K., Germany and France, in Chew, D. H. (ed.) *Studies in international corporate finance and governance systems: a comparison of the U.S., Japan and Europe.* Oxford University Press, New York, pp. 281–296.

Friedman, M. 1962. *Capitalism and freedom.* The University of Chicago Press, Chicago.

Friedman, M. 1970. The social responsibility of business is to increase its profits. *The New York Times Magazine,* September 13.

Frith, B. 1997. BHP crisis puts spotlight on the role of Beswick block. *The Australian,* August 13, 1997, p. 22.

Frith, B. 1998. It's time referee blew whistle on BHP's Beswick. *The Australian,* September 22, 1998, p. 22.

Garnaut, J. 2008. China's sharemarket stability goes on the run. *The Sydney Morning Herad,* April 21, 2008, p. 1, 24.

Gatti, C. and Mouawad, J. 2007. *Chevron seen settling case on Iraq oil.* Available: http://www.nytimes.com/2007/05/08/business/08chevron.html, accessed March 24, 2008.

Global Reporting Initiative 2008. What We Do. Available: http://www.globalreporting.org/AboutGRI/WhatWeDo/, accessed January 28, 2008.

Goodman, D. S. G. 1994. *Deng Xiaoping and the Chinese revolution.* Routledge, London.

Green, S. 2004. *The development of China's stock market, 1984–2002: equity politics and market institutions.* RoutledgeCurzon, London.

Hackett, S. C. 1998. *Environmental and natural resources economics: theory, policy, and the sustainable society.* M. E. Sharpe, Armonk, NY.

Haigh, G. 1987. *The battle for BHP.* Information Australia with Allen & Unwin Australia, Melbourne.

Hancock, J. (ed.) 2005. *Investing in corporate social responsibility: a guide to best practice, business planning & the UK's leading companies.* Kogan Page Limited, Sterling.

Hartcher, P. 2007. *Global 100 national champions.* Available: http://www.thediplomat.com/article.aspx?aeid=2714, accessed May 17, 2008.

Hawkins, D. E. 2006. *Corporate social responsibility: balancing tomorrow's sustainability and today's profitability.* Palgrave Macmillan, New York.

Ho, B. 2008. *CSR as "No. 1" issues for state-owned enterprises in China.* Available: http://www.csr-asia.com/upload/csrasiaweeklyvol4week02.pdf, accessed February 16, 2008.

Hobbs, R. 2000. *Chapter 10, corporate governance, board structure and accountability,* ESRC Centre for Business Research, University of Cambridge. Available: http://www.dti.gov.uk/cld/nov2000/ch10nov.pdf, accessed May 10, 2004.

Hopt, K. J. 1998. The German two-tier board: experience, theories, reforms, in Hopt, K. J., Kanda, H., Roe, M. J., Wymeersch, E. and Prigge, S. (eds.) *Comparative corporate governance: the state of the art and emerging research,* Oxford University Press, New York, pp. 227–258.

Horstman, M. 1997. BHP strikes in Dominica. *Multinational Monitor,* vol. 17, no. 9, pp. 6–7.

Hoshi, T. 1998. Japanese corporate governance as a system, in Hopt, K. J., Kanda, H., Roe, M. J., Wymeersch, E. and Prigge, S. (eds.) *Comparative corporate governance: the state of the art and emerging research.* Oxford University Press, New York, pp. 847–875.

Hoshi, T. and Kashyap, A. K. 2001. *Corporate financing and governance in Japan: the road to the future.* MIT Press, Cambridge, MA.

Howarth, S. 1997. *A century in oil: the "Shell" transport and trading company 1897–1997.* Weidenfeld & Nicolson, London.

Hu, R. 2007. *Governance of state-controlled listed companies in China: the current situation and policy suggestions.* Available: http://www.oecd.org/dataoecd/18/51/39303186.pdf, accessed June 1, 2008.

Hutton, J. 2008. *China and UK: partners in sustainability.* Available: http://www.berr.gov.uk/pressroom/Speeches/page45691.html, accessed April 21, 2008.

Hyland, A. 2008. China's $17bn mine-feeding frenzy. *The Australian Financial Review,* April 14, 2008, p. 6.

Imhof, A. 1996. The big, ugly Australian goes to Ok Tedi. *Multinational Monitor,* March, pp. 15–17.

Information Office of the State Council of the People's Republic of China 2007. *China's energy conditions and policies.* Available: http://english.people.com.cn/90001/90776/90785/6327632.html, accessed December 27, 2007.

Insiderinvestment 2008. Insiderinvestment. *Ethical Performance,* vol. 9, no. 10, pp. 10.

Jensen, M. C. and Meckling, W. H. 1976. Theory of the firm: managerial behavior, agency cost, and ownership structure. *Journal of Financial Economics*, vol. 3, no. 4, pp. 305–360.

Jia, X. 2004. Corporate governance and corporate social responsibility in China: past, present and future. *Australian Journal of Corporate Law*, vol. 17, no. 1, pp. 136–143.

Jiang, Q. 2002. *Standardizing behavior and deepening reform, to be creditworthy and responsible shareholders of listed companies: speech at the meeting on summarizing the experience of establishing modern enterprise system in listed companies (abstract)*. Available: http://www.setc.gov.cn/english/setc_engl/qygg_eng/qygg_0022.htm, accessed February 7, 2004.

Kanda, H. 1998. Comparative corporate governance country report: Japan, in Hopt, K. J., Kanda, H., Roe, M. J., Wymeersch, E. and Prigge, S. (eds.) *Comparative corporate governance: the state of the art and emerging research*. Oxford University Press, Oxford, pp. 921–942.

Karliner, J. 1997. *The corporate planet: ecology and politics in the age of globalization*. Sierra Club Books, San Francisco.

Kaye, T. 1994. Beswick parcel draws ASA flak. *The Sydney Morning Herald*, July 6, 1994, p. 39.

Kaye, T. 2003, Judging by more than the cover–Australasian reporting awards-corporate governance. *The Australian*, May 23, 2003.

Kemp, S. 2003. DLCs sap shareholders: report. *The Age*, September 30, 2003, p. 1.

Kennedy, D. 1996. Ok Tedi all over again: Placer and the Porgera gold mine. *Multinational Monitor*, vol. 17, no. 3, pp. 22–24.

Keri, G. 2004. Bullish companies bounce back. *Asiamoney*, vol. 14, no. 10, pp. 43–50.

Kiel, G. C. and Nicholson, G. J. 2003. Board composition and corporate performance: how the Australian experience informs contrasting theories of corporate governance. *Corporate Governance*, vol. 11, no. 3, pp. 189–205.

Klare, M. T. 2001a. The new geography of conflict. *Foreign Affairs*, vol. 80, no. 3, pp. 49–61.

Klare, M. T. 2001b. *Resource wars: the new landscape of global conflict*. Metropolitan Books, New York.

Kohler, A. 2000. Only Rio Tinto could get away with it. *The Australian Financial Review*, May 30, 2000, p. 19.

Kohler, A. 2001. Peace in our time. *The Australian Financial Review*, March 3, 2001, p. 21.

Korporaal, G. 2007. Door open to China buy-ups, says Rudd. *The Australian*, October 5, 2007, p. 1, 21.

Le Billon, P. 2001. The political ecology of war: natural resources and armed conflicts. *Political Geography*, vol. 20, pp. 561–584.

Le Billon, P. 2005. *Fuelling war: natural resources and armed conflict*. Routledge, New York.

Lee, S. L. J. 2008. From non-tradable to tradable shares: split share structure reform of China's listed companies. *Journal of Corporate Law Studies*, vol. 8, no. 1, pp. 57–78.

Lewis, S. and Armitage, C. 2005. Beijing deal a price cut bonanza. *The Australian*, April 20, 2005, p. 1.

lexmercatoria.org 1997. *China—Company Law, 1993*. Available: http://www.jus.uio.no/lm/china.company.law.1993/portrait, accessed May 17, 2008

Li, R. 2003. *Welcome to the website of the State-owned Assets Supervision and Administration Commission of the State Council (SASAC)*. Available: http://www.sasac.gov.cn/eng/zrzc.htm, accessed August 22, 2004.

Li, Z. 2007. *A structural problem of corporate governance in China.* Available: http://www.oecd.org/dataoecd/19/33/39302836.pdf, accessed May 31, 2008.

Lin, J. 2003. *Zhenjianhui Xiuding Nianbao Pilu Zhunze, Qianshida Liutong Gudong Xu Xianshen (CSRC revised the rules for annual report disclosure, the largest 10 tradeable shareholders have to be disclosed),* http://www.cnstock. com. Available: http://www.finance.sina.com.cn/roll/20031224/0623574481. shtml, accessed February 19, 2004.

Lin, J., Zhou, N., Levine, M. D. and Fridley, D. 2006. *Achieving China's target for energy intensity reduction in 2010: an exploration of recent trends and possible future scenarios.* Available: http://china.lbl.gov/publications/lbnl-61800. pdf, accessed December 25, 2007.

Liu, G. and Sun, P. 2005. The class of shareholdings and its impacts on corporate performance: a case of state shareholding composition in Chinese public corporations. *Corporate Governance: An International Review,* vol. 13, no. 1, pp. 46–59.

Long, S. 2000a. Rio Tinto spurns union line. *The Australian Financial Review,* March 9, 2000, p. 4.

Long, S. 2000b. Top five nominee funds in Rio Tinto ordered to name their investors. *The Australian Financial Review,* May 1, 2000, p. 5.

Long, S. 2000c. Unions give themselves the high-fives. *The Australian Financial Review,* May 25, 2000, p. 24.

Long, S. 2000d. Unions launch global attack on Rio board. *The Australian Financial Review,* March 8, 2000, p. 1.

Long, S. and Oldfield, S. 2001. Unions step up merger fight. *The Australian Financial Review,* May 11, 2001, p. 63.

Lux, J., Thorsen, S. S. and Meisling, A. 2005. The European initiatives, in Mullerat, R. (ed.) *Corporate social responsibility: the corporate governance of the 21st century.* Kluwer Law International, Boston.

Maiden, M. 2007. Chinese move on Nufarm opens a two-way street for Australian businesses. *The Age,* November 6, 2007, p. 1, 12.

Manne, H. 1965. Mergers and the market for corporate control. *The Journal of Political Economy,* vol. 73, no. 2, pp. 110–120.

Manning, P. 2003. Business-poor mining industry. *The Sydney Morning Herald,* April 18, 2003, p. 43.

Markoff, J. 2007. China's US drive stirs disquiet. *The Australian Financial Review,* August 28, 2007, p. 35.

Mayer, C. 1994. Stock-markets, financial institutions, and corporate performance, in Dimsdale, N. and Prevezer, M. (eds.) *Capital markets and corporate governance.* Clarendon Press, Oxford, pp. 179–194.

McCarthy, J. 2000. Union dons new garb to move into boardroom. *The Courier-Mail,* May 22, 2000, p. 15.

McCreary, E. I. 1996. *China's energy: a forecast to 2015.* Available: http://www. lanl.gov/orgs/d/d4/pdf/china.summary.pdf.

McIlwraith, I. 1993. BHP plays smart with Beswick. *Australian Financial Review,* January 5, 1993, p. 28.

Medjad, K. 2006. In search of the "hard law": judicial activism and international corporate social responsibility, in Allouche, J. (ed.) *Corporate social responsibility.* Palgrave Macmillan, New York.

Milhaupt, C. J. and West, M. D. 2004. *Economic organizations and corporate governance in Japan: the impact of formal and informal rules.* Oxford University Press, Oxford.

Monks, R. A. G. and Minow, N. 2001. *Corporate governance,* 2nd. Blackwell Publishers, Malden, MA.

Mullerat, R. (ed.) 2005. *Corporate social responsibility: the corporate governance of the 21st century*. Kluwer Law International, Boston.

Newell, R. 2008. *China investment boom masks governance risks—report*. Available: http://responsible-investor.com/home/article/china/, accessed April 5, 2008.

Ng, P., Curtain, R. and Nadarajah, S. 2004. The top 500. *Business Review Weekly*, vol. 26, no. 16, April 29, 2004, pp. 64–73.

Nolan, P. 2001. *China and the global economy: national champions, industrial policy and the big business revolution*. Palgrave, Basingstoke, Hampshire.

OECD 2001. *Corporate social responsibility: partners for progress*. OECD, Paris.

OECD 2007. *Cost of pollution in China: economic estimates of physical damages*. The World Bank. Available: http://siteresources.worldbank.org/INTEAPREG-TOPENVIRONMENT/Resources/China_Cost_of_Pollution.pdf, accessed December 27, 2007.

Okabe, M. 2002. *Cross shareholdings in Japan: a new unified perspective of the economic system*. Edward Elgar Publishers, Northampton, MA.

People's Daily Online 2001. *China's securities market to show characteristics of internationalization*. Available: http://english.peopledaily.com.cn/english/200103/20/eng20010320_65459.html, accessed May 21, 2005.

People's Daily Online 2005a. *51 listed central SOEs undertake split equity structure reform*. Available: http://english.peopledaily.com.cn/200512/16/eng20051226_230767.html, accessed January 13, 2006.

People's Daily Online 2005b. *China launches 2nd round of experiments to tackle major capital market problem*. Available: http://english.peopledaily.com.cn/200506/20/print20050620_191139.html, accessed June 25, 2005.

People's Daily Online 2005c. *China selects firms for experiments to tackle major problem facing sluggish stock markets*. Available: http://english.peopledaily.com.cn/200505/10/print20050510_184242.html, accessed June 25, 2005.

People's Daily Online 2005d. *Direct election of grass roots trade union leaders burgeons*. Available: http://www.english.peopledaily.com.cn/200505/09/print20050509_184068.html, accessed June 25, 2005.

People's Republic of China 2005. *The Company Law of the People's Republic of China (revised in 2005)*. Available: http://wzj.saic.gov.cn/pub/ShowContent.asp?CH=ZCFG&ID=213&myRandom=.93876781826, accessed May 24, 2008.

Pheasant, B. 1998. Beware: directors in danger. *The Australian Financial Review*, July 4, 1998, p. 26.

Proctor, G. and Miles, L. 2002. *Corporate governance*. Cavendish, London.

Psaros, J. 2003. Objective measures will beat any rhetoric. *Australian Financial Review*, December 4, 2003, p. 63.

Psaros, J. and Seamer, M. 2002. *Horwath 2002 corporate governance report*. Available: http://www.ecgi.org/codes/country_documents/australia/horwath_cg_02.pdf, accessed September 24, 2004.

Pukthuanthong, K. and Walker, T. 2007. Venture capital in China: a culture shock for Western investors. *Management Decision*, vol. 45, no. 4, pp. 708–731.

Ren, X. 2005. More than 400 firms started split structure reform; the total market value of tradable shares now reached 40 million Yuan (Gugai Gongsi yi you Sibai Jia, Liutong Shizhi Yida Siqian Yi). *Securities Daily*, December 25, 2005.

RepuTex 2003. *RepuTex summary rating report: BHP Billiton Ltd.* Available: http://www.reputex.com.au/pdfs/2003Summary_split/bhp.pdf, accessed October 6, 2004.

Reuters 2007. Shenhua Energy looks offshore to satisfy appetite. *The Australian Financial Review*, December 7, 2007, p. 53.

Richardson, B. J. 2002. *Environmental regulation through financial organisations: comparative perspectives on the industrialised nations*. Kluwer Law International, London.

Rio Tinto 2003a. *2003 report to the community: Lihir Gold Limted*. Available: http://www.riotinto.com/investor/information/socrecinv/reporting.aspx, accessed November 8, 2004.

Rio Tinto 2003b. *Coal & Allied 2003 social and environmental report*. Available: http://www.riotinto.com/investor/information/socrecinv/reporting.aspx, accessed November 8, 2004.

Rio Tinto 2003c. *Rio Tinto publishes the following policies and guidance*. Available: http://www.riotinto.com/investor/information/socrecinv/reporting.aspx, accessed November 2, 2004.

Rio Tinto 2004a. *History*. Available: http://www.riotinto.com/aboutus/history.aspx, accessed September 27, 2004.

Rio Tinto 2004b. *Rio Tinto 2003 annual report and financial statements*. Available: http://www.riotinto.com/investor/information/analystInfo/default.aspx, accessed October 11, 2004.

Rio Tinto 2007. *Rio Tinto 2007 annual report*. Available: http://www.riotinto.com/investors/reports.asp?searchKeyword1=year%202007, accessed June 9, 2008.

Rio Tinto 2008a. *Chairman and executive directors*. Available: http://www.riotinto.com/whoweare/216_board.asp, accessed June 9, 2008.

Rio Tinto 2008b. *Features*. Available: http://www.riotinto.com/ourapproach/217_features_6712.asp, accessed June 10, 2008.

Rio Tinto 2008c. *Management overview*. Available: http://www.riotinto.com/whoweare/management_overview.asp, accessed June 9, 2008.

Rio Tinto 2008d. *Our products*. Available: http://www.riotinto.com/whatweproduce/218_our_products.asp, accessed June 9, 2008.

Rio Tinto 2008e. *Rio Tinto 2007 general purpose financial report*. Available: http://www.riotinto.com/investors/reports.asp?searchKeyword1=year%202007, accessed June 9, 2008.

Rio Tinto 2008f. *Sustainable development*. Available: http://www.riotinto.com/investors/219_sustainable_development.asp, accessed June 10, 2008.

Rio Tinto 2008g. *The way we work*. Available: http://www.riotinto.com/documents/ReportsPublications/the_way_we_work.pdf, accessed June 9, 2008.

Roe, M. J. 1994. *Strong managers, weak owners: the political roots of American corporate finance*. Princeton University Press, Princeton, NJ.

Rose, J. 2001. Welcome to the new corporate culture. *The Australian Financial Review*, March 29, 2001, p. 35.

Ross, M. L. 2004. What do we know about natural resources and civil war. *Journal of Peace Research*, vol. 41, no. 3, pp. 337–56.

Sakuma, K. 2001. Japan, in Gugler, K. (ed.) *Corporate governance and economic performance*. Oxford University Press, Oxford.

Salsbury, S. and Sweeney, K. 1988. *The bull, the bear and the Kangaroo: the history of the Sydney Stock Exchange*. Allen & Unwin, Sydney.

Sampson, A. 1975. *The seven sisters*. Hodder and Stoughton, London.

Schipani, C. A. and Liu, J. 2002. Corporate governance in China: then and now. *Columbia Business Law Review*, vol. 2002, no. 1, pp. 1–69.

Schutt, D., Buerkle, T., Capon, A., Dini, J., Gopinath, D., Hamlin, K. and Lanchner, D. 2001. China—Asian role model? *Institutional Investor-International Edition*, vol. 26, no. 11, pp. 14.

Senate Select Committee on Securities and Exchange 1974. *Australian securities markets and their regulation*. Australian Government Publishing Service, Canberra.

Shell 2004. *Unification of Royal Dutch and Shell Transport*. Available: http://www.unification.shell.com/shell_proposal/general/proposals/press2/, accessed May 6, 2008.

Shell 2005. *Shell global scenarios to 2025: the future business environment: trends, trade-offs and choices.* Shell International Limited, London.

Shell 2008a. *At a glance: business.* Available: http://www.shell.com/home/content/aboutshell-en/at_a_glance/at_a_glance_09112006.html, accessed May 4, 2008.

Shell 2008b. *At a glance: overview.* Available: http://www.shell.com/home/content/aboutshell-en/at_a_glance/at_a_glance_09112006.html, accessed May 4, 2008.

Shell 2008c. *The beginnings.* Available: http://www.shell.com/home/content/aboutshell-en/who_we_are/our_history/the_beginnings/the_beginnings_history_of_shell_22112006.html, accessed May 4, 2008.

Shell 2008d. *The board of Royal Dutch Shell plc.* Available: http://www.annualreportandform20f.shell.com/2007/reportofthedirectors/boardofdirectors.php, accessed May 10, 2008.

Shell 2008e. *Environment and society.* Available: http://www.shell.com/home/content/envirosoc-en?LN=/leftnavs/zzz_lhn1_0_0.html, accessed May 10, 2008.

Shell 2008f. *Shell Energy Scenarios to 2050 with Jeremy Bentham.* Available: http://www.shelldialogues.com/shell-energy-scenarios-to-2050, accessed May 10, 2008.

Shell 2008g. *What we do.* Available: http://www.shell.com/home/content/aboutshell-en/what_we_do/dir_what_we_do_07112006.html, accessed May 10, 2008.

Sinopec Corp. 2005. *Sinopec Interim Report 2005.* Available: http://english.sinopec.com/en-ir/en-companyreport/index.shtml, accessed January 21, 2006.

Sinopec Corp. 2007. *Sinopec 2007 annual report.* Available: http://english.sinopec.com/download_center/reports/2007/20080406/download/AnnualReport2007.pdf.

Sinopec Corp. 2001. *Interim Report 2001.* Available: http://english.sinopec.com/en-ir/en-companyreport/index.shtml, accessed February 12, 2005.

Sinopec Corp. 2003. *2002 Annual Report.* Available: http://english.sinopec.com/en-ir/en-companyreport/index.shtml, accessed February 12, 2005.

Sinopec Corp. 2004a. *2003 Annual Report.* Available: http://english.sinopec.com/en-ir/en-companyreport/index.shtml, accessed February 12, 2005.

Sinopec Corp. 2004b. *Composition.* Available: http://english.sinopec.com/en-ir/en-governance/en-governoverview/1338.shtml, accessed February 21, 2005.

Sinopec Corp. 2004c. *Corporate overview.* Available: http://english.sinopec.com/en-company/938.shtml, accessed February 11, 2005.

Sinopec Corp. 2004d. *Interim Report 2004.* Available: http://english.sinopec.com/en-ir/en-companyreport/index.shtml, accessed February 12, 2005.

Sinopec Corp. 2004e. *Sinopec Corp. to Privatize Beijing Yanhua.* Available: http://english.sinopec.com/en-newsevent/en-news/2241.shtml, accessed February 15, 2005.

Sinopec Shanghai Petrochemical Company Limited 2003. *Sinopec Shanghai Petrochemical Company Limited 2002 Annual Report.* Available: http://www.spc-ir.com.hk/eng/report.asp, accessed December 23, 2003.

SIRAN 2008. *Sustainability reporting in emerging markets: an analysis of the sustainability reporting in selected sectors of seven emerging market countries.* Available: http://www.siran.org/pdfs/SIRAN-KLD_Report_for_EM_Transparency_2007.pdf, accessed January 28, 2008.

Smil, V. 1993. *China's environmental crisis: an inquiry into the limits of national development.* M. E. Sharpe, Armonk, NY.

Smith, S. 1998. BHP to dismantle Beswick. *Herald Sun,* December 19, 1998, p. 83.

Standards Australia 1996. *AS/NZS ISO 14001:1996.* Standards Australia, Homebush, NSW.

Standards Australia 2003. *AS 8003–2003: corporate social responsibility.* Standards Australia International, Sydney.

Stanford 2000. *Chevron.* Available: http://www.stanford.edu/group/SICD/Chevron/chevron.html, accessed March 24, 2008.

Stapledon, G. P. 1996a. *Institutional shareholders and corporate governance.* Clarendon Press, New York.

State-owned Assets Supervision and Administration Commission of the State Council 2004. *Zhuyao Zhize (Main Duties).* Available: http://www.sasac.gov.cn/zyzz.htm, accessed August 21, 2004.

State Economic and Trade Commission. *Introduction of the State Economic and Trade Commission, PRC.* Available: http://www.setc.gov.cn/english/index_e.htm, accessed February 11, 2005.

Streeck, W. and Yamamura, K. 2003. Introduction: covergence or diversity? Stability and change in German and Japanese capitalism, in Yamamura, K. and Streeck, W. (eds.) *The end of diversity? Prospects for German and Japanese capitalism,* Cornell University Press, Ithaca, pp. 1–50.

Su, P. 2005. *Sheng Yue Yong was publicly criticised about the loan to the dominant share holder.* Available: http://finance.sina.com.cn/stock/s/20050524/00081614659.shtml, accessed September 16, 2005.

Sutherland, T. 2008. Sinosteel gets approval to buy Murchison stake. *The Australian Financial Review,* September 22, 2008, p. 3.

Sykes, T. 1978. *The money miners: Australia's mining boom 1969–1970.* Wildcat Press, Sydney.

Sykes, T. 1994. *The bold riders: behind Australia's corporate collapses.* Allen & Unwin, Sydney.

Tam, O. K. 1999. *The development of corporate governance in China.* Edward Elgar Publishers, Northampton, MA.

Tan, W. 2008. *Sinosteel strides toward takeover.* Available: http://www.bjreview.com.cn/business/txt/2008–05/10/content_115941.htm, accessed May 17, 2008.

Taylor, L. 2008. *Swan OKs China's Rio Tinto stake.* Available: http://www.theaustralian.news.com.au/story/0, 25197, 24235125–601, 00.html, accessed September 7, 2008.

Taylor, L. and Ryan, C. 2005. China wants incentives to buy Australian resources. *The Australian Financial Review,* April 26, 2005, pp. 1, 4.

TCL Communication Equipment Corporation Limited 2003. *TCL Communication Equipment Co., Ltd. 2002 annual report (in Chinese).* Huizhou, Guangdong Province.

The Australasian Institute of Mining and Metallurgy 2004. *2004 the AusImm public policy platform.* Available: http://www.ausimm.com/policy/platform.pdf, accessed January 30, 2005.

The Australian 2004a. 40 years of business—40 years of the Australian. *The Australian,* July 28, 2004, p. 1.

The Australian 2004b. Australasian reporting awards—corporate governance–business survey series. *The Australian,* May 21, 2004, p. 1.

The Australian 2008. Top 100. *The Australian,* November 21, 2008, p. 1, 29.

The Economist 2008. The lucky country. *The Economist,* vol. 386, no. 8571, pp. 10–12.

The Global Fund 2008. Chevron is first "corporate champion." *Ethical Performance,* vol. 9, no. 10, pp. 3.

The HIH Royal Commission 2003. *The failure of HIH Insurance: a corporate collapse and its lessons.* Commonwealth of Australia, Canberra.

The State Council of China 2004. *Some opinions of the State Council on promoting the reform, opening and steady growth of capital markets.* Available: http://www.lawinfochina.com/law/displayModeTwo.asp?id=3366&keyword=, accessed May 23, 2009.

The United Nations 2007. *What is the UN Global Compact?* Available: http://www. unglobalcompact.org/AboutTheGC/index.html, accessed January 28, 2008.

Theisen, M. R. 1998. Empirical evidence and economic comments on board structure in Germany, in Hopt, K. J., Kanda, H., Roe, M. J., Wymeersch, E. and Prigge, S. (eds.) *Comparative corporate governance: the state of the art and emerging research.* Oxford University Press, New York, pp. 259–265.

Tilburn, J. 2002. *Corporate terminator: a do-it-yourself on corporate governance.* Bookhouse, Sydney.

Tingle, L. 2007. Ore ownership a thorny issue for Rudd. *The Australian Financial Review,* December 7, 2007, p. 83.

Tomasic, R. 2005. Comparing corporate governance principles: China, Australia and OECD, in Tomasic, R., Wang, F., Zhao, X. and Ma, Z. (ed.) *Corporate governance: challenges for China.* Law Press, Beijing, pp. 1–32.

Tomasic, R. and Andrews, N. 2007. Minority shareholder protection in China's top 100 listed companies. *Australian Journal of Asian Law,* vol. 9, no. 1, pp. 88–119.

Tomasic, R. and Bottomley, S. 1993. *Directing the top 500: corporate governance and accountability in Australian companies.* Allen & Unwin, St. Leonards, NSW.

Tomasic, R. and Fu, J. 1999. The Securities Law of the People's Republic of China: an overview. *Australian Journal of Corporate Law,* vol. 10, no. 3, pp. 268–289.

Tong, X. 2005. *Financial services in China: the past, present and future of a changing industry.* China Knowledge Press Private Limited, Singapore.

United Nations 2005. *Global summit: China.* Available: http://www.unglobalcompact.org/docs/news_events/8.1/China_Summit_Final_Report.pdf, accessed January 28, 2008.

Uren, D. 2007. *China emerges as our biggest trade partner.* Available: http://www. theaustralian.news.com.au/story/0, 20867, 21674786–2702, 00.html, accessed April 13, 2008.

Vaughan, M. 2008. Chinese move on Abra opens up more mining buys. *The Australian Financial Review,* May 14, 2008, p. 20.

Wang, M. 2004. The Independent Directorship System in China. *Australian Journal of Corporate Law,* vol. 17, no. 2, pp. 243–259.

Wei, Y. 2003. *Comparative corporate governance: a Chinese perspective.* Kluwer Law International, London.

Weissman, R. 1997. Remember Shell, boycott Shell. *Multinational Monitor,* vol. 18, no. 12, pp. 5.

West, R. 1974. British multinational in hot water. *Business and Society Review,* vol. Spring 75, no. 13, pp. 76–79.

Wilson, N. 2007. China wins its first Aussie oil acreage. *The Australian,* August 1, 2007, p. 1, 32.

Wilson, W. 1998. *Making environmental laws work: an Anglo American comparison.* Hart Publishing, Oxford.

Wood, L. 1999. Beswick buyback will boost BHP, says report. *The Age,* January 26, 1999, p. 1.

World Bank 2003. *Corporate governance: an issue of global concern,* World Bank. Available: http://www.worldbank.org/html/fpd/privatesector/cg/aboutus.htm, accessed March 14, 2003.

World Bank 2007. *East Asia remains robust despite US slow down.* Available: http://web.worldbank.org/WBSITE/EXTERNAL/COUNTRIES/EASTASIAPACIFICEXT/CHINAEXTN/0, , contentMDK:21550665~menuPK:318956~pagePK:2865066~piPK:2865079~theSitePK:318950, 00.html, accessed January 6, 2008.

World Business Council for Sustainable Development 2008. *WBCSD member companies.* Available: http://www.wbcsd.org/web/about/europe.htm, accessed May 10, 2008.

Xinhua News Agency 2008. *Overview of the eleventh five year plan*—[Online, in Chinese]. Available: http://news.xinhuanet.com/ziliao/2006–01/16/content_4057926.htm, accessed April 13, 2008.

Yahoo 2006. *Shanghai Baosteel Group Corporation Company Profile*. Available: http://biz.yahoo.com/ic/57/57074.html, accessed January 20, 2006.

Yakovleva, N. 2005. *Corporate social responsibility in the mining industries*. Ashgate, Aldershot, Hants, England.

Ye, X. 2004. Shell sells holdings in second-largest oil firm. *China Daily*, March 19, 2004, p. 10.

Yergin, D. 1993. *The prize: the epic quest for oil, money and power*. Pocket Books, New York.

Yi, X. 2008. *Stock market's faults must be addressed*. Available: http://www.chinadaily.com.cn/opinion/2008–03/27/content_6568792.htm, accessed April 13, 2008.

Zerk, J. A. 2006. *Multinationals and corporate social responsibility: limitations and opportunities in international law*. Cambridge University Press, Cambridge.

Zhang, J. 2004. *Catch-up and competitiveness in China*. RoutledgeCurzon, London.

Zhou, D., Levine, M. D., Dai, Y., Yu, C., Guo, Y., Sinton, J. E., Lewis, J. I. and Zhu, Y. 2003. *China's sustainable energy future: scenarios of energy and carbon emissions (summary)*. Available: http://china.lbl.gov/publications/scenarios_summary_01apr04.pdf, accessed December 25, 2007.

Zhu, R. 2002. *Report on the work of the government (full text) (16/03/2002)*. Available: http://www.fmprc.gov.cn/eng/topics/3701/3702/t18930.htm, accessed August 30, 2004.

Zonneveldt, M. 2007. China's uranium rush—NT prospects excite resources-hungry giant. *The Courier-Mail*, January 13, 2007, p. 1, 66.

Zweig, D. and Bi, J. 2005. China's global hunt for energy. *Foreign Affairs*, vol. 84, no. 5, pp. 25–38.

About the Authors

Dr. Xinting Jia is an Associate at the Responsible Investment Unit of Mercer Investment Consulting; previously she worked at the Centre for International Corporate Governance Research of Victoria University in Australia and remains as an Adjunct Fellow of the Centre.

Professor Roman Tomasic is the Chair in Company Law at Durham University in the United Kingdom and previously worked on this project at Victoria University in Australia.

Index

Printed in the United States
by Baker & Taylor Publisher Services